Life with My Schizophrenic Father

Sandra L. Wyllie

This book is dedicated in the memory of my father Anthony Angelo Palladino.

Please feel free to contact me at: leeann827@hotmail.com

We are all the same. We're born. We die. We just do different stuff while we're waiting.

People think love is complicated; but it really isn't. All you need to love is to love. It's that simple.

Table of Contents

Wrap Yourself Up

in my arms
they're the blanket
to your soul
throw out all your troubles
allow them to float
weightless in the air
lay your weary head
upon my chest
close your eyes
drift away
slumber in peace
ensconce in my arms
nothing can get to you
no one can do you harm
swaddled in my love
my breath a gentle breeze
rocks you in a cradle
of elongated limbs
nestles you in comfort
before another day begins

Rest in peace, father

Anthony A. Palladino   12/29/32 -2/19/04

Chapter 1

You Know He's Not Right

"You know he's not right". That's all I ever heard from my mother growing up when daddy used to go into his psychotic rages. I had no one to turn to as an only child when daddy got mad at the world. He thought people were out to destroy us. He would refuse dinner at times thinking that even my mother had poisoned the food. I would be so terrified when he would look under the car for hidden bombs and put nickels on top of all the door ledges to see if anyone had tried to break in. If the door moved the nickel would have fallen off the narrow space of the ledge.

We were always living on the razor's edge. My mother used to yell at me because I would cry and get frightened. She always blamed me for making her life more difficult. I was just a very scared little girl that felt totally unsafe fearing that at any time someone would kill me or my daddy for sure.

I grew up at 1431 Centre St. in Roslindale, Massachusetts, a suburb of Boston. I lived in a two-family gray house with black trim. My parents bought it from my father's father, Angelo Anthony Palladino. He named his son, my father, after him, calling him instead Anthony Angelo. He was the only child from his father's second marriage to a woman named Sophie. Sophie had a child (a son) out of wedlock as a teenager and gave that child up for adoption. There was great shame in those days for a woman to raise a baby when she was unwed.

My father had five half- sisters and one half- brother from his father's first marriage. I don't know much about that union except for the fact that his first wife was mentally ill and died in an institution for the insane. Mental illness ran high on my father's side of the family.

1

Life with My Schizophrenic Father

My father was born on December 29, 1932. He grew up during the great depression, where people couldn't afford money for food and often, sadly lived in their cars. Herbert Hoover was in the white house awaiting Franklin Roosevelt's presidency. My father grew up in a two-family brown house on 1435 Centre St. in Roslindale, only two houses over from the house he would live in after I was born.

He lived on the second floor along with four half- sisters, Helen, Rosy, Edith and Mary and a half-brother, named Philly. His other half- sister Constance lived on the first-floor apartment of that house after she married her husband Charlie. She is still alive to this day at the ripe old age of one hundred and four and is still living in the house. Her husband has long since passed and they never had any children.

My father had always said he felt like the black sheep of the family. The other kids despised him because their father married another woman. My father was the product of that union. Of course, my grandmother was saddled with raising all her husband's children from his first marriage. This was extremely difficult on a young woman only in her twenties to be newly married with an instant family of six kids.

You Know He's Not Right

My grandmother always lived in shame because of her first-born son that she had to give up. She didn't wear a veil in her wedding pictures because she wasn't virginal when she married. As a result, she would never allow me to see her wedding pictures. She never talked about her other son, nor did my father. I only found out about him much later.

My father attended Roslindale High School. After he graduated in 1950, he joined the army. He was stationed in Japan during the Korean War. I was very interested and very proud of all his army stories. He told me he was an MP, which stood for military police. I thought wow, my dad was a cop! But my father wasn't getting too much action arresting people. He got more action from a very special Japanese woman with whom he fell in love with.

He wanted to bring her back home, but in those days, it was unheard of to have mixed marriages. He knew his family would never approve. So, he left his heart in Japan. But he never forgot her. They kept in touch through mail for a while. One day he got a letter from her telling him that she was pregnant with his child. She was asking him for money so she could "take care of it". I'll never know what really happened. I always wondered if I had a half Japanese sibling out there.

Life with My Schizophrenic Father

My mother only got as far as an eighth-grade education. She came from a family of five. She had three sisters and one brother. Her mother died when she was only fifteen, and she supported herself most of her life working in a factory stitching shoes on an assembly line. Her father was sick and living with his daughters Irene and Mary. My mother was getting divorced from her first husband Tommy Guzzi after seven years of marriage when she met my father.

She met my father at a piano bar where she would often sing. My mother had a lovely voice. She sang quite often in the house. She told me she and her sisters used to harmonize when they did the dishes at night. At the time my parents met my father was working for GE. My father was a shipper. He used to ship packages out to different parts of the world. "Volare" was their song, by Dean Martin.....

"Volare, oh, oh! Cantare, oh, oh, oh, oh!
Let's fly way up to the clouds, away from the maddening crowds
We can sing in the glow of a star that I know of
Where lovers enjoy peace of mind
Let us leave the confusion and all disillusion behind
Just like birds of a feather a rainbow together we'll find"

My mother never knew about my father's illness while they were dating. He was dashingly handsome, with jet black curly hair and a very lean body and olive skin. My mother was equally beautiful with her big, doe brown eyes and svelte figure. She wore her auburn hair high up in a big beehive, which was popular back in the 60's.

You Know He's Not Right

Both of my parents smoked. My father smoked Camels and my mother smoked Parliament cigarettes. Later on, my father switched to Lucky Strikes. My mother did a lot for my father when they were dating. She got him to go to Bentley College for accounting. She got him to buy a car. My father was a compulsive gambler. He went through money fast. I remember him taking me to Suffolk Downs racetrack when I was little to watch the horse's race. And I went with him to casino nights long before there was ever a Foxwoods or Mohegan Sun.

My parents got married by justice of the peace and had their reception at his old family home in the basement that his half-sister Constance was occupying. The year was 1962.My mother's sister Emma was her matron of honor. And my father's half -brother Philly was his best man. The basement was furnished with a full bar. My aunt loved to entertain.

My parents moved to a small apartment on Kittredge St. in Roslindale when they first got married. It was another multiple family home, like the one my father grew up in. They met their best friends there, the Magistri's. They were a young Italian couple struggling to make ends meet. The wife Sherry became fast friends with my mother. She stayed home with her little daughter Mary while her husband Gerry worked all day and attended night school. My mother was the only one who was not Italian in the bunch. She was English and Portuguese. Her maiden name was Pinero.

Life with My Schizophrenic Father

Eventually my parents moved to a small white house on Concreve St. in Roslindale and Sherry and Gerry bought a house in Hudson when they were expecting their second child Jerry. The white house on Congreve Street that they rented was owned by Katherine Spileos. She had a son Andrew, who was a couple of years older than me. My mom became friends with her as well. My mom actually conceived me and I was born while they lived at that house. But my parents moved to the two-family on Centre St. when I was only a couple of months old.

My father's half-brother Philly lived on the second floor apartment with his son Steven (from his first marriage) and his second wife Maria. Steven's new home now is in Cedar Junction prison in Walpole for running one of the biggest Ponzi scams since Ponzi himself. He robbed many doctors' blind of their retirement so he wouldn't have to work and could live the life of a millionaire. At this time my grandfather Angelo owned the house before my parents bought it from him when I became a teenager. My parents were only renting the first-floor apartment.

Steven's mother Josie died of breast cancer when Steven was just a small child. And he despised his stepmother Maria. Maria had three daughters from her first marriage. Two of those daughters were always over the house visiting and Steven felt like a third wheel so much so that he eventually moved to my father's childhood home two houses over on 1435 Centre after my grandfather died.

You Know He's Not Right

My mother left her job when I was born to stay home and take care of me. She was the model housewife, keeping an immaculate house, cooking and baking all the time. We used to have three course meals of stuffed mushrooms and artichokes, lamb and pasta, with homemade meatballs and braciole, which is a thin slice of meat with fillings such as eggs and breadcrumbs, wrapped inside it and rolled up. Lemon meringue and apple pies along with chocolate cake were often served for dessert. My father used to love to eat even though he never gained a pound. He would buy the best prosciutto (Italian ham) that was twenty dollar a pound. Our house always wafted of delectable aromas.

I was born July 11, 1965, as Sandra Lee Palladino. For some strange reason my mother nick-named me buttercup. We were in the middle of the Vietnam War and there was still a lot of racial tension between the blacks and the whites. Just a few months after I was born the big blackout of the northeast had occurred. It went as far north as Ontario, Canada, all the way down the east coast, as far as Pennsylvania. My mother was all alone at home with me currently. Everyone was without electricity for thirteen hours.

The strain of being a new mother and my father's illness was starting to take its toll on my mother at this time. Mental illness ran high on my father's side of the family. My father's half-sister Helen had such severe depression that she needed electric shock treatments that left her in "a child-like state" for the rest of her life. Her son, my cousin Johnny also had schizophrenia.

Life with My Schizophrenic Father

Schizophrenia is a long-term severe brain disorder involving a breakdown in the relation between thought, emotion, and behavior, leading to faulty perception, inappropriate actions and feelings, withdrawal from reality and personal relationships into fantasy and delusion, and a sense of mental fragmentation.

During this time my father lost his job at GE because of his severe paranoia. He was having delusions and hearing voices. He had names for these voices. The one in his left ear was called "Dreddrew" the one in his right ear was called "Shaddrack". These voices used to tell him horrible things.

People with schizophrenia can resort to suicide or murder if the voices tell them to do so. Many are hospitalized for the illness and are put on anti-psychotic drugs to maintain the symptoms, which can have ruinous effects on their lives and on those of their loved ones.

At this point my father was also drinking and gambling heavy. He was nearing his first mental breakdown. My mother couldn't tolerate all his accusations and delusions. One of his delusions was that my mother had an affair with my cousin Johnny. He thought that I was the product of that affair, and that I was not his daughter but Johnny's daughter instead, which until his death in 2004 he supported.

You Know He's Not Right

My parents separated when I was only a couple of years old. My mother started dating a politician. She was bitter and angry about this becoming another failed marriage just liked her first and she took that out on me. There was one incident that stands out in particular. She wanted to wash her kitchen floor. She always had such an immaculate home. She didn't want me to interfere, so she locked me outside on the porch while she attended to this task.

I knocked on the door to come in. She refused to let me in, refused to even let me come in the back hallway. I was stubborn, even way back then. I didn't want to stay on the porch. So, I banged my head on the glass door for her to open it up. She swore some profanities, like she always did call me a "cock-sucker" and telling me to go "fuck yourself". Well I wouldn't stop and eventually I pounded my head so much that my whole head broke right through the glass. It was amazing that I wasn't seriously injured.

She was furious. She got a hold of me and took down my pants and beat me so hard that I was bleeding and had welts on my bottom. This was clearly child abuse at its best.
From then on things got worse and worse with her. My father said that he felt so bad coming by one day (during their separation) to pick me up. He looked in the window and saw me sitting forlorn at the kitchen table while my mother was getting dressed to go out on a date. My father felt doubly betrayed because he saw his own mother there waiting to babysit me while my mother went out with another man.

Life with My Schizophrenic Father

Despite the mental anguish that my father was going through at this time we were very close. He came to get me every weekend to go horseback riding and out to dinner. There was a small farm we used to go to in Milton that had horses and you could ride them in the corral. We also used to go to Larz Anderson Park to feed the ducks. I remember these times fondly. My father was a very soft-spoken man when he was with me. And although he never believed I was his daughter or showed me any outward affection I knew from his actions that he loved me very deeply.

Around this time, I was introduced to my nemesis, Rebecca Kettel. She was the only daughter of my mother's friend Sally. My mother met Sally when she used to go over to visit her in-laws (two houses down from where we lived). Sally, a divorced mother raising three boys and a daughter all on her own while working full-time at Children's Hospital in the radiology department rented the house next door to my grandparents. Sally had a lot in common with my mother. They had hard upbringings, were divorced and had truck-driver mouths, weren't afraid to tell anyone to "fuck-off" either.

Sally ended up moving a few houses up across the same street from us. And my mother took a job babysitting her four kids, including Rebecca when they came home from school. Rebecca was only a year younger than me, blonde, blue-eyed and beautiful. My mother took a shining to her immediately.

You know He's Not Right

My father had his first mental breakdown during my parent's separation. He was out of work and drinking heavy and full of paranoid delusion. He would think words on the radio were encrypted code coming through from the CIA or the FBI warning of sabotage. He was also gambling excessively ever last dime of his money. He was completely broke and despondent when he begged my mother to take him back. He came in the house rolling on the floor like a child screaming and clutching his throbbing head. It must have been like a nightmare for him to never be able to shut off the voices that screamed at his brain. My mother felt total pity for him, so she reluctantly took him back.

My father was committed to McLean. McLean is a mental health hospital in Belmont, just eight miles from downtown Boston. Some very famous people stayed at McLean like James Taylor, Ray Charles and Steven Tyler from the band Aerosmith. The hospital is ranked the second best of all psychiatric hospitals in the country.

My father started seeing the psychiatrist Dr. Robert Torchin, who had a private office in Newton. Decades later after my father passed away I would get to meet Dr. Torchin when I became his patient myself. My father was prescribed the ant-psychotic drug stalazine. With the help of Dr. Torchin and stalazine he slowly started to stabilize. But my father's schizophrenia would haunt him for the rest of his

Chapter 2

My Early Childhood

 I was an extremely shy and insecure child. The first few years
until grade four I attended Longfellow Elementary School in
Roslindale. The building is still there, but now it's a section
eight public housing for the low-income elderly. My
grandmother or Aunt Helen (who lived on the street right across
from us on Ardale used to pick me up every day from school.
Aunt Helen suffered severe depression. She had electric shock
treatments that left her in such a state that she was always slow
and child-like in manner.

Aunt Helen had an illegitimate son Johnny who also suffered
schizophrenia. He and my cousin Steven were very close. I was
only close to Steven because he lived in the same house as me
(on the second floor) and was only eight years older than me. I
remember hanging out with him at my grandmother's house on
Saturday mornings watching the Saturday morning cartoons Fat
Albert and the Cosby kids and The Jackson 5ive.

I knew all of Steven's girlfriends, from his first tender sweet
long, dark haired Rose, to the very shy one who looked like
princess Dianna and had my name, Sandra. Steven was just like
the brother I never had. We even had nicknames for each other.
He called me "shrimp" because I was small and I called him
"punk", which is ironic because that's what he turned into.

Life with My Schizophrenic Father

My mother became more and more abusive. If I spilled a glass of milk, she would go into a psychotic frenzy screaming obscenities at me. All she cared about was that her house was immaculate. If I didn't obey my mother, she would beat me with a metal spatula. She used to chase me around the dining room table with that spatula. If I didn't clean my room enough to her liking or pick up my toys, she would either break them or throw them away. She would get into a psychotic rage screaming "this house looks like tobacco road." The real Tobacco Road is a historic tobacco producing area of North Carolina.

During this time, she was getting closer and closer to Rebecca, since she was baby-sitting for her five days a week. If that wasn't enough Rebecca would come over on the weekends as well. My mother made me share everything with her. I remember when my mother made roasted lamb. We always used to fight over the leg which had the most tender meat on it. I felt like an outsider. I was always in the shadows. I never existed outside of them until after both of my parent's deaths when I was in my late thirties.

My father would run hot and cold. One day he could seem like a perfectly normal father and then the next day he could be ranting and raving like a lunatic. I was very frightened of both of my parents. It's a terrible shame for a little girl to be frightened all the time with no explanation of what was going on around her. I remember my mother pleading with Dr. Torchin on the phone. I heard his name brought up all the time in my house.

My Early Childhood

No one ever really knew the private hell I was living in because my parents displayed a different façade to the outside world. Some of my friends thought I was so lucky to have a mother that cooked and baked home-made meals all the time. And they never saw my father's dark side. My parents had a horrible marriage. My mother would claw my father with her long, red nails leaving rather large scratch marks on him that would openly bleed, much like a feral cat would do if you tried to pick it up.

After the fourth grade I transferred over to Holy Name School in West Roxbury. This was a catholic school that was run by nuns. I met my childhood friend Nancy Williams there. She lived on the same street as me, just a few houses up. I used to love going over her house. It felt like "Ozzie and Harriet" when I visited her. She had an older sister and brother. Her mother was warm and kind. She had her own playroom, aside from the bedroom she shared with her sister. And her mother always made hot lunches for us. Life at the Williams seemed like all-American and normal. Little did they know what I was dealing with in my own private hell.

I was very manipulative of Nancy. I didn't want her to have any other friends except me. She seemed like my only salvation. I became very jealous when she became friends with this outgoing girl named Elaine who lived on Ardale Street, the same street my aunt Helen lived on, except further up. I guess I wanted to be the focal point in Nancy's life of normalcy. It's kind of funny because she lived directly across the street from my arch rival Rebecca.

Life with My Schizophrenic Father

My father got a job at Lambert's Silk-screening company
working in the shipping department. He carpooled so he could
save wear and tear on his car. My mother always had dinner on
the table exactly five thirty every night after he came home from
work, with dessert afterward. My mother made me eat foods that
I hated until I threw up. I particularly hated squash. I got wise
and used to hide discarded food in my napkin. They both
smoked after dinner. And I sat on either side of them, so I got
the brunt of all the toxic chemicals in the air. I had no choice but
to inhale them. This turned me off cigarettes. As a result, I never
took up smoking.

My parents used to argue at the dinner table all the time. It
would usually start as soon as my father walked in the house
looking tired and sullen after working all day. My mother's first
intrusive question would be "Why do you have that puss on your
face?" Of course, my father would say nothing and ask what's
for dinner, because that's all he cared about. Then a fight would
ensue and there would be lots of screaming and swearing. My
mother was good at throwing things. Of course, I was always
caught in the middle of it. So, I learned to eat really fast and
retreat to my bedroom.
Besides I didn't want to hear my father talking, what my mother
called "ragtime", another name for his paranoid delusional
thinking.

My Early Childhood

I had a rich fantasy life to escape my tumultuous home life, and that included masturbation. I masturbated at a very young age. My mother always tried to discourage me with name calling saying I was a disgusting pig and slut. My mother hated men and sex. My father told me she never wanted sex and use to just lie there and ask "is it over yet". My mother always told me "men will chew you up and spit you out.

I used to suck my fingers, the pointer and the middle one put together. I never sucked my thumb. I always did things differently than the other kids. I also used to rock myself back and forth in a full body rolling motion every night just to get to sleep. If I didn't do this repetitive motion, I wouldn't be able to fall asleep. I didn't quit this behavior until I was twelve years old. As with most things in my life I just stopped doing it one day and never needed to do it again.

I was pretty much a loner except for my friendship with Nancy. I would try to hide when people came over to visit. I was extremely shy and never wanted to see anyone. I even peed in my bedroom closet one time when Rebecca came up so as not to have to see her and my mother chatting it up smoking like two teenage girlfriends. I felt just like a misfit. I didn't belong in this world. I'm still that way, even now to this day. The difference is now I embrace it.

Life with My Schizophrenic Father

The next psychotic break my father had I vividly remember. It was my thirteenth birthday. Is it no coincidence that thirteen is an unlucky number? Well it sure was for me. My parents took me out for a lobster dinner at The Red Coach Grill restaurant on route 9 in Newton. It's no longer there anymore. The restaurant had a big sign of a stagecoach pulled by horses out in front of it.

All was quiet during dinner. It's when we got back home that things began to shift. My father had paranoid delusions about my uncle Charlie. Charlie was a janitor at the hotel Marriot in Boston. His wife Connie (who was my father's half-sister) worked in the kitchen of that hotel. They both lived on the first floor of the two-family home on 1435 Centre St. My grandparents and my aunt Edith lived on the second floor.

Charlie used to be a boxer in his younger day. He loved to smoke cigars and pipes. He loved to go fishing too. I remember him taking me one time. We had to leave really early, like at five in the morning. I was surprised that the fish would even be awake at this time. But it was fun. We got some good fish that day and brought them home for my aunt Connie to cook up for dinner. Charlie was a very quiet man. He never had much to say. He certainly didn't seem like the argumentative type, so I don't know what happened between him and my father on my thirteenth birthday. But all hell broke loose.

My Early Childhood

After dinner my father started talking ragtime again. This time he started saying crazy things about my uncle. He was headed over to his house (which was only two houses over) and was on a rampage. He started pounding on his door. My mother and I followed closely behind. I was starting to get really scared. I didn't understand, like always when these episodes occurred, what exactly was going on. My father started screaming obscenities at my uncle Charlie and it looked like he was ready to punch him.

My aunt took me inside and locked my father out. He was still screaming obscenities and pounding on the door even more vehemently than he was before. Aunt Connie brought me into the guest bedroom and told me that I would be staying there for the night. I started crying and trembling. It was my birthday after all, and this was not how I wanted it to end. After dinner we should have been eating cake and ice cream. I should have been opening up my presents. But sadly, this is not the way the events of that day would unfold.

I blocked out all memory of what happened after this. I have blocked out a good chunk of my early childhood. I am only now starting to recover it after twelve years of therapy. I think I dissociated a lot during these times because it became too painful to deal with. But it has left a severe emotional scar on me. I myself have been diagnosed as having borderline personality disorder. I also have suffered severe anxiety attacks and social phobias all through my life.

Life with My Schizophrenic Father

Borderline Personality Disorder is a mental illness that is marked by a chronic pattern of unstable relationships, poor self-image, and mood changes. It is also characterized by severe impulsivity. Borderlines have black/white and all/nothing thinking. There are no shades of grey for them. They either love you or hate you. They split off their feelings. The way I can describe this illness is if a normal person gets a scratch it is no big deal. To a borderline a scratch becomes a gaping wound gushing with blood. When they feel they feel intensely, or else they dissociate and not feel at all.

Also, my social phobia's always left me paralyzed and having crippling anxiety attacks when I was around people. Therefore, I became a loner. People "wrote off "this behavior as many things. Some thought I was a stuck-up snob because I wouldn't attend family get togethers or other social events. Some thought that I was just shy. Some thought that I didn't like them. The truth was none of these. And unless you suffer this illness, you'll never know what it is truly like.

The anxiety attacks were severe. I felt like I couldn't breathe and that I was dying. I had severe dizzy spells all the time. I used to worry about the dizzy spells because my mother's sister Emma, died of a brain tumor in her fifties. My heart would race so much I thought that I was having a heart attack. I would sweat profusely, get flustered and red in the face. It was just horrible going through life like this.

My Early Childhood

I didn't do well in school. In fact, I was picked on a lot. There was this huge, tall fat girl that always bothered me. I was a little petite thing. You could blow me over without taking a deep breath. Back then no one talked about bullying. It wasn't recognized as it is today. So, I couldn't get any reprieve, either at school or at home. My life was a living hell and I had no one to turn to. To this day I have blocked out most of the pain of my childhood. I cannot recall in detail all the abuse that I have endured. I am currently working on that in my therapy, with my two therapists. One I have been seeing for free for the past twelve years, the other one goes through the traditional insurance.

My father never hit me or even raised his voice to me all my life. He never showed affectionate to me either. He never hugged me or told me that he loved me. Yet I was still very close to him except when he would have his psychotic breaks. My father was a very patient man. He would listen for hours on end to me talk about almost anything and everything. I used to sit crisscross /apple sauce beside him on his bed while he was lying under the covers many nights. I would talk about the teachers I had crushes on and the many schemes as a kid I would plan. No matter how crazy my stories were or no matter how tired he grew from the heavy medication he was on he always listened with interest to me. I will never forget those special moments with him.

Life with My Schizophrenic Father

My father had a great sense of humor. We would laugh our heads off all the time. This infuriated my mother. She was very jealous of our close relationship. I had a lot of good times with my father. We both loved to sing that song by Gloria Estefan "Bad Boys" which drove my mother crazy. My father used to take me to Wollaston beach in Quincy in the summer. We would get fried clams at the clam shack across the street. And we went miniature golfing during the summer evenings. My mother never went anywhere with us. We never did anything together as a family.

One time when we went miniature golfing, I found a baby frog. My father let me bring him back home. I wanted to keep him as a pet, even though I already had a French poodle named Rene. My father was a pushover as always and couldn't say no when he saw how excited I got over catching that frog. I put him in a box. Of course, the next day my mother threw him out and lied as she told me that his mother (the frogs) came all the way from the golf course to our house to take her baby back home. I was a very gullible kid, so I bought that absurd story, until years later when she told me the truth.

I loved going out to dinner with my father because he loved to eat. We both loved Italian food. We would leave my mother at home then too. My mother never liked going out to restaurants, that way she couldn't bitch about how long and how hard she slaved over a hot stove all day. She loved to play the martyr.

Chapter 3

The High School Years

After Holy Name I went to St. Clare High School on Cummings Highway in Roslindale. It's no longer there now. Another school has taken its place. I made three new friends there, Maria, who was Italian like me, Cheryl and Julia. My relationship with Nancy was waning. She was a year behind me and still at Holy Name. She had also started making many new friends, herself.

My father was a great taxi driver to me and my girlfriends. He drove me to school every day. He ended up driving both Nancy and Rebecca to St. Clare as well when they started a year later. He drove Cheryl and me to all the Red Sox games. Cheryl and I had crushes on some of the ballplayers. We used to wait for them outside the stadium after the game for autographs. One time we even followed one to a local bar. We were underage so we couldn't go into the bar. We only could salivate outside of it and hold on tight to our young girl dreams. But I used to write some of them, and they would write me back. My favorite was the pitcher Steve Crawford.

My mother never drove. She never even got her license. All she did was cook and clean and babysit during my high school years. And by baby-sitting, I mean she made the kids sleep all day and when they were awake she had them propped up in front of a television. She would put the kid's coats on and take them outside for a minute and then lie to their parents telling them she took them out for the afternoon.

Life with My Schizophrenic Father

My father taught me how to drive by taking me to the cemetery every weekend and letting me get behind the wheel of his two door, green Plymouth Duster. He was very patient with me. If I did a good job, he would allow me to drive the car home. I still went to the driver's school in West Roxbury. I needed all the help I could get. I flunked my first driver's test in Norwood by backing up into the curb. I still don't know how to back up straight! My son Austin printed up a sign for me that hangs on my refrigerator that says "when people talk about my driving.......... But did you die?"

I have a very special memory of my father and me during a Red Sox game one summer. This time I went to the ballgame without Cheryl. It was just my father and me. We got there early and walked down from our seats to get a closer look at the players practicing. The Sox's where playing the Oakland A's. Rob Picciolo was up at bat. He hit the ball and it came straight to where we were standing behind home plate. I put my hand out to catch it. I did catch it too!! Unfortunately, professional baseball players hit those balls pretty hard and I wasn't wearing a glove for protection. It felt like a bullet was shot into my hand. I dropped the ball and reeled in severe pain from catching it with my bare hands. Rob saw what happened and rushed over to see if I was ok. He autographed the ball and handed it to my father. It was worth the pain. I'll never forget that day!

The High School Years

My sophomore year of high school I had a major league crush on my geometry teacher Mr. Richard Moche. He later became a lawyer. Most of the girls had a crush on Mr. Timmons, who was blonde haired, rugged and athletic looking. I, on the other hand liked Mr. Moche who had black curly hair and a scruffy beard, was not athletic looking, and was more of a goofball. I always had different taste than the other girls. I always liked older men too.

Cheryl and I were in the school's variety show that year. That meant we had access to the school in the evenings when we went there for practice. By nature, I'm a snoop. I like to look and go into places where I don't belong. So, during a break from rehearsal I went into the teacher's lounge. I happened to find a book with a list of the teacher's names and their contacts in it. They had a contact number for Mr. Moche. It wasn't his phone number listed in it, but a person someone could call if there was an emergency involving Mr. Moche.

I went home all excited and told my dad that I wanted him to call that contact number and ask for Mr. Moche's home number. Back then nobody had cell phones. My dad was hesitant at first. He told me that he didn't know how to ask, or what to say. I told him just tell the person that you're an old college friend of his and want to get in touch with him again. My dad called and said what I told him to say and it worked like a charm! My dad could never say no to me. And he was always in cahoots with me. I got Mr. Moche's home number. Of course, I called him (incognito) and we talked. He was real nice on the phone, especially since he didn't know who he was talking to.

Life with My Schizophrenic Father

My father used to talk about the days when he was a young child suffering from scarlet fever. He was put in solitary confinement in a hospital ward and not allowed any visitors. It's a horrible thing for a child to be sick all alone. That was a very traumatic and scary experience for him to go through. He told me that what he remembers about it was how the nurse used to shake down the thermometer each time before and after she took his temperature. That nurse must have been a welcome companion for a poor child locked up all alone.

This reminds me of the beautiful children's story by Margery Williams "The Velveteen Rabbit". In the story the boy becomes sick with scarlet fever and all his toys have to be thrown away because they've become contaminated. What a horrible experience for a child to go through. It makes me wonder if this contributed to my dad's schizophrenia. My dad already felt ostracized enough as a boy growing up in a household with half siblings, all belonging to another woman. They always made sure to treat my father like not only an outsider, but an outcast as well. I'm sure this illness only isolated him more. He must have really felt abandoned. It is a time in his life that he never got over.

The High School Years

There were two times in high school were I almost got expelled. I was always a crazy kid pulling pranks. I used to tape the pages of my Latin teacher's book together. That was for a good laugh. The next day when she came to class, she couldn't turn the page. I would always be doing dumb things that got me into trouble. In fact, in my high school year book "High Way 1983" I was voted by all my peers as the ZOOIEST, along with Chris Zept. I must give her credit here as well.

The first major, really dumb thing I did was to bring a genuine pig to school. No, it wasn't for show and tell or to be used for the classroom pet. The poor thing was cramped in my pocketbook all morning until I let him out at lunch time. And when I say I let him out I mean it literally. I was showing him off to another student when he got loose in the high school cafeteria during the height of our lunch. He was running up and down the aisles. Everyone was screaming. Of course, this brought attention to the nuns. And when they found out that it was mine, I got hauled into the principal's office and they called my mother.

I didn't get suspended but I got detention for many weeks. I wanted a pet genuine pig, but my mother refused. Of course, even to this day I never take "no" for an answer. I always end up doing just what I want to do. I knew if I had left that little critter back home in my room my mother would find it for sure. She always went through my stuff. I never had any privacy.

Life with My Schizophrenic Father

Though I never went to parties or even my prom in high school I did drink. I was a closet drinker, which is the worst kind. I think I had two sides. The very shy girl that people saw on the outside and the wild reckless girl that loved sex and good times that my mother tried to smother. I never got to really know who I was until my late forties, early fifties.

I stayed up all night and drank a bottle of wine one time during my senior year. I was stone drunk when I went to school the next morning. My mother knew I drank the bottle of wine and still sent me to school totally intoxicated. The principal had to call her and tell her to come and collect a very drunken me. I went home and slept it off. Boy did I get into very big trouble for that one!

There was a time I played hooky from school. I just dropped out of school for two weeks. It was in my senior year then too. I almost didn't graduate with my class over that one. I was tired of school and just decided that I didn't want to go anymore. I was a rebel, even back then. But nobody saw me as that way because I was always so quiet and shy. But I always did my own thing, and no one could stand in my way, not even my mother.

The High School Years

I tried cigarettes, but I never inhaled them. I think I just wanted to be cool. I liked cigars because you could smoke them without inhaling. I wanted to try pot, but I chickened out at the last minute. Alcohol has always been my drug of choice.

I didn't have a typewriter so Maria always typed my papers up for me. Her mother used to cook all day on Sunday. Italians have their big dinner on Sunday afternoons. Back then the Blue Laws were in effect and nothing was opened on Sundays anyway, so all one could do was eat, drink and visit relatives.

When I grew up times were very different. If I wanted to talk in private, I had to pull the telephone cord all the way into my bedroom from the kitchen. I stretched the damn hell out of that thing. We had one rotary phone in the house. The kind you got to put your finger in and go all the way around dialing in the number. I did have a TV in my bedroom though, and a stereo. But other than that, I didn't have much else. I inherited all my clothes from my mother's best friend Sherry. Her daughter would outgrow them and then pass them along to me.

My mother forced me into getting a part time job my senior year. So my aunt Edith who worked at the Jewish Rehab Center on our street got me an interview. All the kids from high school worked there after school. And all the kids used to watch General Hospital at three o'clock every afternoon. Everyone had to know the latest details about Luke and Laura and the Ice Princess.

I didn't do well on that job from the rehab. In fact, I hated it. I was doing menial work in the kitchen. I only lasted a couple of months because my grades were slipping. So, I just up and quit like I do with most things when I've reached my end. At this time during senior year everyone was applying for colleges. I wanted to go to Notre Dame College in New Hampshire, which was a Roman Catholic college that used to be exclusively for woman. My mother tried very hard to discourage me from this.

I just wanted to run away from home, really. I used to hear all those commercials on TV. Around this time there was a jingle that would go something like this "When you 've got it bad, we've got it good. Come to Florida". I loved that jingle because I always had it bad. I don't know why I picked a college in New Hampshire since I despise the cold. I got accepted to it though, but unfortunately didn't go. My parents talked me out of it. Both my friends Maria and Julia were going to this community college, Mass Bay in Wellesley Hills. But I just ended up going there with Julia because Maria took a job instead. And Cheryl went to nursing school.

Mass Bay was much cheaper than St. Clare, so my parents both liked that idea. But it wasn't a four-year college. My parents were not big on education. The only thing my mother wanted me to do in life was to get married and have children.

The High School Years

I got my very first kiss when I was eighteen, the summer I graduated from high school. We didn't do anything special, like a party, but my mother took me to Montreal instead. It was a weekend bus trip. Of course, my father didn't go. He never went on vacations with us. I met this boy who was somewhat slow. He worked at the Dunkin Donuts in Everett. His name was Eric and he had never kissed a girl either. I was determined to get my very first kiss out of him on this trip.

After going to an all-girl catholic high school overrun by nuns, I felt that it was time I got to know boys my own age instead of always having crushes on older men. So one night after an evening show we went to see I grabbed Eric and went off somewhere alone and planted my first kiss on him. It wasn't that bad considering it was the first time for the both of us. I must say that it appeared liked he knew what he was doing. The kiss kind of ended up in a semi-make out session. It wasn't just one kiss. But we weren't groping each other either. We just stuck to the kissing. I got his number and called him after the trip, but nothing became of it.

In the fall I would be headed off with Julia to Mass Bay College. It was a co-ed college. Maybe, finally I might meet some boys and have a semi-normal teen-age life. I was nervous but very excited as well too. Mass Bay here I come!!

Chapter 4

Mass Bay

Mass Bay was totally different than St. Clare. There were boys everywhere, lots of them. Julia's sister's best friend Carol drove us there every day until Julia got her own car. Her sister's friend worked just up the highway from the college. When it came time to fill out what courses we were going to take I was stumped. I knew I wanted a higher education, but I wasn't exactly sure just in what.

I followed Julia's lead and took up all the courses she was taking. She majored in Early Childhood Education, so that's what I majored in too. And since my mother baby-sat for young kids it just looked like I was following in her footsteps (barf, gag). My father told me that I was taking "basket weaving" . The courses were simple. St. Clare High seemed much more like college than the courses I was taking here. At St. Clare I took up subjects like Latin, Chemistry, French, Geometry, and Algebra.

My courses at Mass Bay were basic simple math, racquetball (if you can actually believe that!) early childhood ed, general first aid, English and other very simple stuff. It was a total breeze. I ended up nicknaming the college "Mass Bay High". Not only did I ace all my classes, but I got so bored I actually sat in on other more intellectual classes. We also got to work in the field we were in (without pay) as part of the requirements for the associates degree that I received. This is sort of like the co-op that they do at Northeastern University. That way there you get some experience in your field of study as well.

Life with My Schizophrenic Father

Life was fun at Mass Bay. I didn't make any new friends, but Julia did. She met a girl named Ruth when she took a job at the Auto/Visual Center to help pay for some of her college tuition. Ruth was friends with Kenny, who was friends with this boy named Andrew. Little did I know that Andrew would one day become my future husband.

I spent most of my time studying in the dark auditorium of the college. I was a loner and not too many people walked through there. I only saw two people. Since there was a piano on the stage a boy came and practiced on it sometimes. And my English professor Kevin Plunkett walked through there to get to his office. I had a major league crush on professor Plunkett. Of course, he was much older and married with a son. Again, even though the school had lots of boys my own age I fell for the much older man.

The boy (I forget his name) that played the piano told me I needed to get out of that dark auditorium if I was ever to meet people. He said the only friends I could make in there were the paintings hanging on the walls. So he invited me to lunch with a group of his friends. And I went, even though I felt awkward and shy. His parting words to me were to go to places like the library and the audio/visual center (where Julia worked) to study instead of sitting all alone in a darkened auditorium. It was the best advice anyone had ever given to me. I started hanging out at the A.V. center and I met Julia's friend Ruth, who was a hoot! She was a free spirit. Julia also introduced me to some other people, who were boys!!!!!!!!!! She introduced me to Kenny, Paul and Andrew. She said they were all planning on getting together for lunch and asked me if I wanted to join the group. So, I ended up going.

Out of the four people that were going to join us, Ruth
and Andrew were the only two that attended. Andrew was the
chauffer of choice. Ruth sat in the front with him while Julia and
I sat in the back of his blue Chevy Nova. Andrew looked like
John Denver to me. He had poker straight dirty blonde hair and
wore wide framed circle glasses. He was a country boy from
Walpole. He wasn't too refined wearing short-sleeved t-shirts in
the winter with jeans and sneakers. He smelled of old spice
after-shave. And you could tell he used an electric razor to shave
because his face wasn't completely smooth. He also kept a
picture of his parents in his wallet.

Ruth was a wild child who looked just like Irene Cara from the
hit "Fame". She adjusted the review mirror on Andrew's car to
"check her looks". This infuriated Julia because it was
dangerous driving without Andrew being able to see behind him
in that mirror. It was just like Ruth to say, "everything's
groovy". We ended up going to McDonald's. We were college
kids and didn't have much money. I sat down and reserved the
table. Andrew was the first one to come back with his food. Ah,
the smell of disheveled grease. The only other thing Andrew ate
besides McDonald's was those apple fruit-filled pies loaded with
preservatives and high in cholesterol that came wrapped up in
green packaging at the college.

I got to talk to this strange boy because we were all alone for a
few minutes. I thought he looked a bit odd and he stuttered quite
a lot. You could tell that he had no experience around girls. It's
for this reason alone that I was always attracted to older men.
But what could I do, chase after my very married college
professor? I knew I needed to get my head out of the clouds and
find someone my own age.

After that lunch Andrew asked me out on a date. He was the only boy to ever ask me out in my life. So, we planned on going to Fun and Games, which was an arcade place on route nine, not far from the college. He came to my house to pick me up. My father's first impression of him was that he looked just liked Dilly Dally from the Howdy Doody show. Of course, I had no idea who that was. It was well before my time. I dressed up far too formal for the occasion. After all it was only an arcade. And I had on a skirt and a blouse. It might have been an arcade, but it also happened to be my very first date.

I envisioned first dates to be going out to dinner in the evening. But what did I know, since I never dated before. Andrew was a year older than me and still a virgin like me and very wet behind the ears like me. We had a lot in common, back then. When we got to the arcade it was very loud and crowded inside. There was not much to do together except play air hockey, and there's only so many air hockey games you can play. So, we left and he ended up taking me to Bird Park in his home town of Walpole. We enjoyed a nice leisurely walk. It was a beautiful, warm spring day.

I was foolish enough after the park to ask to see his home and his parents. The park was very close to his house. I can't imagine knowing my social anxieties, why I ever even asked this of him, but he agreed. He lived in a small russet ranch house. He was the youngest of four brothers. Two of them had already moved out. That would be Steven, who was married and David who was single. Gary still lived there at the time but was engaged to be married soon.

Andrew's parents seemed friendly enough. His mother, who was called "Bunny" (her real name was Phyllis), was a secretary, and his father, Bruce was a carpenter. His house was situated on over an acre of land with an in-ground swimming pool that included both a diving board and a slide. His family looked so much more normal than mine. I could never tell Andrew about my father's illness or what my mother was really like. I kept all that entirely hidden until after we had children.

Our next date was much more traditional. This time he took me to an evening movie. He picked me up again at my house after dinner. He was dressed really formally with a suit and tie, unlike our last date at the arcade. This time it felt like a real date. The movie was "Splash" starring Tom Hanks and Daryl Hannah. During one of the scenes Daryl Hannah who plays a mermaid kisses Tom Hanks passionately. When Andrew saw this scene, he said "why can't I have a girlfriend like that?" I thought for sure that a kiss would ensue after this date. But sadly, nothing happened. And nothing kept happening date after date thereafter.

So, I asked my girlfriend Julia for advice, since she had many boyfriends. She told me that he might just think that we're "friends" or else he's real shy. I had to find out for sure. I wanted some action. I would be turning nineteen in a couple of months and I only kissed a boy once in my entire life. At this point I wanted sex. I thought by college age that's what people do. And besides that, I was a horny toad!!

Life with My Schizophrenic Father

I even talked to my father about the dilemma I was in. He told me to be patient with Andrew. He said he's a good boy and that it will happen. Yes, he was a good boy. This is one of those circumstances where too much of a good thing can be sexually frustrating!!! One of the kids that we were friendly with at school, a fat, black boy said: "the two of you make the Walton's look like swingers." If you don't know who the Walton's were you won't get that remark. But they were a big, old-fashioned family that lived on a farm in Virginia, with ironically, the oldest boy being a writer (like I would later become).

It turned out that Andrew only kissed one girl before me. We were both so green. When we tried to kiss it was much worse than kissing that slow boy Eric that I met on the bus trip to Montreal. When I kissed Andrew he opened his mouth so wide that we clicked to teeth!! It was a horrible experience. There was no "spark", no magic and certainly no chemistry. But we had a lot in common. And I thought of Andrew as my best friend. Besides, I was ripe for sex.

I wanted to have sex with Andrew. We talked about it and he bought condoms. But when I mentioned this to my mother, she said I was a slut and a whore and that I needed to wait until marriage to have sex. I didn't want to wait. But she kept drilling into my head that he will only gain his experience with me and then eventually dump me. I will become "used goods", like the old adage that says', "why buy the cow when you can get the milk for free". So, I didn't end up having sex then. But I did talk Andrew into marrying me.

I got my first job before I even graduated as a teacher's aide at the Nazareth Seton in Jamaica Plain, working in an all-day class with infants and toddlers. I took my father's Duster to get to work. A few months later Andrew took a job at Stone & Webster Engineering. We planned on getting married after we saved some money, that way I could be virginal and unused just like mommy's dreams. But dear mommy didn't get to have all her dreams come true by this union. She wanted the big catholic wedding at our Holy Name Church in West Roxbury. Andrew was a protestant, was going to remain that way and wanted to raise his kids that way. So I converted to his religion and got married in his church. My mother DID get her beautiful CATHOLIC, "HOLY NAME" wedding when her surrogate daughter, Rebecca got married many years later.

I lost touch with Julia after Mass Bay. I hadn't talked to Cheryl since high school. So, Maria was the only one of my friends to become a bridesmaid. My first cousin Susan was my matron of honor. But I was short one person. Andrew had three groomsmen (his brothers). So, I needed one more to even it out. Guess who I picked? I asked my surrogate sister Rebecca. The big day would be September 12, 1987.

We ended moving in the apartment upstairs in my parent's home. The tenants at the time, Donna and Dennis (a young married couple who had no children) were nicely asked to pack their stuff up and leave. Steven and my Uncle Philly had long moved out. My uncle divorced his second wife and Steven got married to Luanne and bought his own home.

Chapter 5

I Become Mrs. Wyllie

My father did pretty well hiding his illness from Andrew. He had a lot of respect for Andrew, but they did not have much in common. My father was an avid sports fan. Andrew didn't watch sports at all, even though his families, including his mother, were big Patriot fans. Andrew was very serious, and my father liked to joke at very strange stuff, like me. My father always warned me that I didn't chew my wild oats by marrying my first boyfriend. This would later come back to bite me and I would have affairs to make up for those lost years.

I got fired from my job at Nazareth, not because I was a bad worker. It was because I never fit in with the others, and always kept to myself. Aside from that, the woman who used to have my job wanted it back. And they all liked her, so I was out on my ass. I got another job right away though, as a preschool teacher in the "Small Fry" nursery school which was in the West Roxbury YMCA. The director of the preschool program was a woman that was a lot older than me, named Jill. Jill and I were the only teachers of the three classes they held, Monday, Wednesday and Friday, morning class, and then afternoon class. They also had an abbreviated class that ran only twice a week, Tuesdays and Thursdays.

I enjoyed this job much better. I was working with pre-kindergarten children between the ages of three and five, teaching them reading and writing. It was so much better than babysitting for a bunch of whiney toddlers and changing diapers all day like I had to do on my old job.

Life with My Schizophrenic Father

My father used to drive me to my job at the YMCA in the mornings. But he would drop me off an hour earlier so that he could get to his job. We both lived in the same house. I only moved to the upstairs apartment when I got married. We were paying my parents three hundred and fifty dollars for rent a month at the time. But we were both working. My husband took the train to work to get into Boston and parked his car at the station. I would usually walk home from work. It was a good thirty-minute walk.

During the end of the school year the Y replaced the management staff. I was not happy with the new people. I liked the old manager, Bridget. And also Jill started slacking off. She wanted to quit as well to have a baby, even though she wasn't married or dating at the time. She had just broken up with her boyfriend Richie, who was in a rock band. They were pressuring me to take over as the director of the pre-school, since I was very responsible and had been there for several years. I didn't want the responsibility. They were not going to take no for an answer.

I was growing unhappier each day at work. So, I did what any borderline would do. I up and quit without a customary two-week notice. I just wrote a quick note to the new director, left it on his desk one Friday afternoon, walked out and never came back. I sent my father to pick up my last paycheck. Everyone was angry at me, especially my husband Andrew, for leaving that way and not having found another job first. But I didn't really care. I always did exactly what I wanted to do.

I Become Mrs. Wyllie

During this time my grandmother Sophie (my father's mother) became very sick. Both my grandfathers had passed away a long time ago. She had been diagnosed with colon cancer. Her entire colon was removed, and she literally became a "bag lady". She had to wear a colostomy bag to collect her shit since she had no colon. She also had to change and take care of the bag, which became too much for a woman of her age (eighty-three). So, she was placed in a nursing home. This was a very difficult time for my father, seeing his mother rapidly going down-hill.

On the lighter side one of Maria's cats had a litter. So, she asked if I wanted a free kitten. I said yes even though my mother told me when I moved upstairs not to get any pets. But I never listen. So we had a new kitten. And we named him Frank. It was just Frank and I during the day, since I wasn't working. We never had guests, so I cleared the dining room table off and did puzzles all afternoon. I also put on about ten pounds from not working and being lazy all day.

Then the day came shortly after I had left my job that my grandmother had passed away. This was a very depressing and sad time for me. I always feared death, even as a very young person. When my aunt Emma (my mother's sister) died of brain cancer I was too young to grasp what was going on. But this time it really hit me.

Life with My Schizophrenic Father

Andrew told me that Stone & Webster had an opening for an administrative assistant. He thought that he should try to see if he could get me an interview since I wasn't really looking for a job on my own. I had only one interview with a woman who had her own daycare set up at her home. But I didn't get the job. My father implied that Jill "blackballed" me from ever getting a job as a preschool teacher because I walked off my job with her and left her stranded right at the end of the school year. My father was paranoid, but I was starting to believe him. So even though I had no prior experience I went for the interview that Andrew had set up for me at Stone & Webster.

It's kind of funny but my sister-law was working there, along with her father. And my in-laws' best friend was the V.P. of the company. That's how Andrew got his job. And I got the job through Andrew. They told me I could start right away! My father was really proud that I now had a "real job", at an engineering firm, with my own desk and phone and all!! No more "baby-sitting" as he put it. I was kind of proud of myself as well.

I was excited and bought a whole new wardrobe of dresses and skirts, blouses and shoes. I was going to be working around men, engineers!!!! I felt like a kid in a candy shop. At the Y, the youngest guy that I worked with was only five years old! It was pretty cool in the beginning to go into Boston on the train every day with my husband and come home every evening with him.

I Become Mrs. Wyllie

I was making much more money working as an administrative assistant as well. They even paid for their employees to continue their education. Andrew started taking classes at night at Northeastern University to earn his bachelor's degree. He wanted to become a computer programmer. I thought I might try going as well. I took a computer course but was not happy. It just wasn't my thing. I did plan a trip to London for the both of us, though. They had a travel agency right there at Stone & Webster as you entered the building. On my lunch break I went downstairs and booked us a week vacation in London. Andrew was against this because we just came back from Bermuda. I love to travel, which unfortunately is something I no longer do now because of financial reasons. I'm just a starving artist like many of the other ones out there.

At this time working at Stone & Webster I developed two major crushes on two engineers, one was single, the other married. I pursued both of these men. Hossein was the single one from Iran. He had dark, good looks. He was very lean with jet black, wavy hair and a mustache. He was on the small side and he had dark skin as well. Coty was the exact opposite. He was very tall, maybe six foot five. He had light brown hair and a big broad built. He was a country boy, while Hossein was urbanized. Both men were much older than me. I was really into older men. Both men rejected me. There was fortunately no office gossip that I had pursued either one of them. But Andrew knew that I had. I was always honest with Andrew. He was more like my best friend than my husband. And currently, I really didn't have any female friends. Even Maria faded into oblivion shortly after my wedding.

Things took a turn for the worse in the early nineties. Stone & Webster had massive lay offs. And both Andrew and I were given our pink slips. Thank God we lived with my parents because otherwise we would have been homeless since we didn't have the money to pay the rent. I was trying to get pregnant. And when I finally did the pregnancy ended in a miscarriage. I didn't even want to admit that I was having a miscarriage.

But the bleeding and the heavy cramping were undeniable. Then I expelled the whole pregnancy in the toilet. Andrew rushed me off to the Beth Israel emergency room (where I had planned to have the baby). I was in very bad shape. I brought the fetus and the placenta in with me. I had put them in a plastic bag. I don't know why I did this. It was just a knee-jerk reaction I had. Maybe I thought if I brought in the pregnancy the doctors could somehow replant my baby back inside of me.

 The miscarriage left me infertile. I was still bleeding every day for an entire month. I started going to fertility doctors. I was put on the drug clomiphene, which I only got very fat from taking. I went from one hundred and fifteen pounds to one hundred and seventy-five pounds.
I was suffering a severe depression during this time. The miscarriage was devastating. Right before I miscarried, I saw the baby during an ultrasound. And the baby had a strong heartbeat. We had already picked out the name "Sarah Margret" and had bought baby furniture for the nursery. These were some of the darkest years in my life.

I Became Mrs. Wyllie

If that wasn't bad enough, we ended up on welfare. Andrew took a job at the local Stop and Shop. He was barely making minimum wage. He had just finished night school and earned his bachelor's degree. But he still couldn't find a job as a computer programmer. I had pulled our bedroom mattress out onto the living room floor. All the shades were drawn down. I lived in total darkness, like the darkness that was buried deep inside my chest.

We tried doing IUI's (intra-uterine inseminations). The high doses of clomiphene left my mucus impenetrable to sperm. When clomiphene first came out it was intended to be used as birth control, but instead had the opposite effect on woman. It made them even more fertile. My sister-in-law had twins while on that drug. But the drug had the original intent of what it was supposed to do with me. So, in order to bypass my hostile mucus the doctor injected into my vagina Andrew's sperm that had been pre-treated. But that didn't work either. After a couple of tries we gave up. I felt totally inadequate as a woman.

The fertility doctor told me, with a grave face that I will never be able to have children on my own. For the first time in my life I felt really hopeless. I went off the fertility drugs and just gave up. I used to eat and drink to try to numb the severe pain. I wasn't talking to either of my parents. I never went anywhere on the holidays. I became a real recluse. Of course, I heard that my nemesis Rebecca had a baby girl. And guess what she named her? Sarah, the name I had chosen for my miscarried child.

Chapter 6

Welcome Alex

I had a dream one night that really changed my whole life. It was more like a "vision in a dream". I was walking by this house and I saw a statue of the virgin mother Mary outside. The statue was all in white stone. She was in the middle of someone's front yard, with blue and violet flowers surrounding her feet. I stopped and look at her with admiration. Then I started weeping to her that I would never have the baby that I wanted. The statue came to life. She looked up at me with her soft, kind eyes and said only two words that I will never forget to this day. She said; "you will".

Then something amazing happened. After two years of trying to get pregnant, miscarrying and being told by the fertility doctor that I would never have a child on my own I got pregnant! It was like that dream I had really was a way of telling me that it would happen! And it did! I had missed my period. And when I took a pregnancy test it came back positive. I went to the Ob right away to confirm. They gave me a blood test to measure the HCG, which increases greatly during pregnancy. It was true. Then the doctor put me on progesterone to help maintain the pregnancy, since I miscarried before. Progesterone helps build the lining of the uterus.

I took it very easy the entire pregnancy. I ate well, took my prenatal vitamins, never missed an Ob appointment and used the progesterone suppositories I was given. I also took naps every day and watched the O.J. trial, live on tv. It was the summer of 1995.

Life with My Schizophrenic Father

But what should have been the best time of my life, the time I had waited an eternity for and had suffered severe, crippling depression overturned into another nightmare. Around the time Alex was due my father was going through another one of his mental breakdowns. This one was an even worse than the one he had at my thirteen birthday.

My father went off his medication for no apparent reason. He said he didn't need it anymore. This can be a catch-22 because as long as someone is on their medication, they start feeling much better. What some people don't understand is they are much better because they are taking their medication. My father NEEDED his medication to prevent the hallucinations. But the downside of any medication is that it has nasty side-effects. He felt the medication dulled his senses so much that he was like a living zombie. I guess he wanted to "feel again", see the world more sharply.

I certainly couldn't blame my father for feeling this way. He knew he was going to be having a grandson soon. We already named him Alexander Joseph. My father was excited about finally having the boy he always dreamed of. He couldn't wait to take him to all the ballgames. My father was very much into sports. If he wanted to stop his medication, he should have consulted a doctor first. But just like me, my father took things into his own hands. And it turned out to be a total disaster.

Welcome Alex

My father's mental health started to deteriorate rapidly. He was driving my mother crazy with his hallucinations. I'm not exactly sure what was going on because I was staying in my apartment all day trying to de-stress to make sure that I didn't lose this pregnancy. But I knew that something was definitely going on because he moved out of the house again, just like he did when I was a young child. He moved into his half-brother's Philly's house. I also heard rumors that he was being abusive to my mother.

I was trying hard to stay out of all of this because I wanted to maintain a healthy outlook for my upcoming baby Alex. One day during the end of my pregnancy, I didn't feel Alex move at all. This was highly unusually because Alex was like a quarterback inside of me. I could see the outline of his ankle kicking the hell out of me. In fact, I could practically see his whole foot kicking out from my stomach, as if it had a will of its own. Maybe he was trying to score a touchdown. I was so huge that Alex could have been throwing a football in there too without my knowing it! But this day nothing happened. I was worried he might have died inside of me, which does happen to some woman.

I called the doctor and they told me to come in the hospital to do a stress test. They hooked my stomach up to all these wires that were attached to a machine and gave me a gallon of water to drink. Alex was indeed alive. It was that I was just dehydrated from not drinking enough fluid. They made me drink so much that I had to keep getting up to go pee. Now let me tell you this wasn't fun because I had to keep all those wires firmly attached to me. So each trip into the bathroom I had to haul the whole kit and caboodle in with me. They wouldn't stop testing until Alex was moving. That day my boy must have been sleeping very soundly.

Life with My Schizophrenic Father

The day finally came when Alex was born. He didn't enter the world too easily, at least not in my eyes. I was pushing my brains out for three and a half hours. The doctor gave me an episiotomy. They also used a vacuum on his head. And he still ripped me stem to stern. There was so much blood in the room it had looked like a crime scene instead of the birthing of a baby. The day was Sunday, August 27, 1995 when BIG Al made his debut at nine and a half pounds. I was glad the pregnancy was over. It was a scorching, hot summer to be supersized like I was, more than anything on the McDonald's menu! I couldn't even fit in my shoes near the end!

Because of the situation with my father and the estrangement with my mother, neither of my parents attended Alex's baptism. In fact, I had no friends either from all my reclusive years spent in a massive depression. So, there were only two people who attended Alex's baptism. They were Andrew's parents. There was no party or anything afterwards. What should have been the happiest time in my life turned into a very lonely and sad occasion. I topped off at two-hundred pounds when I delivered Alex. And I was still extremely heavy. So, I had a very poor body image as well.

I waited a long time for my baby Alex, but unfortunately it didn't turn out as I expected with no one to really celebrate it with and feeling isolated and all alone. I was going to bottle feed him but I decided to give breast-feeding a chance since my breasts were so engorged and in pain. Breastfeeding relieved that pain. I was very concerned that it would feel sexual because I associated breast sucking as foreplay. But actually, it turned out to be the most enjoyable and peaceful thing I had ever experienced. The breastfeeding prevented my periods from coming back, which was a good thing. I didn't want to go back on the birth control pill again.

Welcome Alex

Andrew got lucky and got a job answering questions on the phone that were computer related. The company would train him to do so. The company was named Stream and it was in Canton. The only downside was that he would have to work the night shift. So, I really wouldn't get much of a chance to see him. I became very lonely in the evenings because Alex would be sleeping, and Andrew would be working. I didn't have anyone to talk to, so I relied on the computer to keep me company.

We had AOL and Yahoo. I used to go into the chat rooms and talk to guys. I would kiddingly enter a chat room by saying: "who wants to have cybersex?" That would get their attention. I was becoming disillusioned with my life, isolated and craving attention. I also wondered what it would be like to be with another man. I was thirty years old, a new mother, and had never been with anyone except my husband. I started making friends with guys on the internet, but nothing came of it at this time.

I was also thinking about whether I wanted to have a second child. It took over three years to have Alex. I did get pregnant on my own, finally. But I was concerned because I was over thirty. I didn't want to stop breastfeeding though, since it was the only thing that brought me peace. As long as I was breastfeeding, I wasn't ovulating or getting periods. I would need to give up breastfeeding in order to try to become pregnant again.

Life with My Schizophrenic Father

When Alex was eighteen months old, I decided to stop breastfeeding him so I could get my periods back. As soon as I stopped my menstrual cycles did indeed resume. So, we attempted to try to get me pregnant. I never imagined in my entire life that I would succeed on the very first try. I was almost thirty-two years old. I figured if I was lucky, I would have the next baby by the time I was thirty-five. After all it took several years to have Alex. It was the day before Easter when I found out that baby Austin was on his way. When we went to see my in-laws at Easter that year (1997) to tell them the good news they were not happy. In fact, my mother-in-law said, very boldly "don't expect us to congratulate you."

Again, what was supposed to be a happy occasion for me turned into something else. I was completely isolated from my parents; had no friends and now my in-laws were very unhappy with the news that Alex was going to have a sibling. They thought that we couldn't afford a second child, and that it was just too soon after Alex's birth to have another baby. I didn't expect we would have another baby so fast.

Alex was becoming a handful. He was always a colicky baby and never slept the night. He would want to be breastfed every hour. But now he threw tantrums all the time. We couldn't go out to dinner with him or take him anywhere. There seemed to be something wrong with him socially as well. We had signed him up for Gymboree to be with other kids. But he wouldn't interact with the other children. He didn't know how to. He was in a world of his own. We would soon find out why.

Chapter 7

Welcome Austin

Compared to Alex, Austin was a breeze. His birth was a piece of cake. He practically delivered himself. I was walking around the maternity ward thirty minutes before he was born. Then I went into my private room and started watching TV. I remember watching a rerun of the comedy show "Eight Is Enough". When my water broke Austin was ready to come out, but the doctor was not ready to deliver him! He was very busy. The nurses kept paging him to come to my room. Austin's head was showing, but the doctor's head sure wasn't! The nurses told me to pant and NOT push, which is what my body wanted to do.

By the time the doctor came, the nurses had to almost rip his sports jacket off of him to prepare him for the birth. He didn't do a thing. Austin flew out all by himself! Alex had paved the way for his little brother. During this time too I got the biggest scare of my life. I knew I was going to breastfeed Austin because I did so successfully with Alex. While I was breastfeeding, I noticed a big lump in my left breast. I was so scared. I told my Ob about it. He gave me the name of a breast surgeon. I just had my second child and thought I had breast cancer and would never live to see either one of my children grow up.

I had the lump checked out right away. It turned out benign. But this problem of getting breast lumps would pop up again and again for me many times.

Life with My Schizophrenic Father

Austin was doing very well. He was sleeping through the night right from the start. He never even cried. He was a very quiet and happy baby, always smiling. In fact, unlike Alex we could take Austin anywhere for any length of time. We used to go on long museum tours, out to restaurants and everything with him. But as much as Austin was doing well Alex was becoming much worse. Alex's pediatrician recommended a complete evaluation at Children's Hospital. This is when we received the devastating new that Alex had autism.

It was very hard to grasp this news. Now I was the mother of a special needs' child with a schizophrenic father and a newborn baby. I also had a lot of emotional problems myself. Things started to get really overwhelming for me. Autism is a mental condition present from early childhood, characterized by difficulties in communicating and forming relationships with other people, and in using language and abstract concepts. That is why Alex never socialized with the other children in his Gymboree class. He would play along beside them without ever interacting with them or even really noticing that they were there. He needed an early intervention program right away.

During this period too Andrew was laid off from his job at Stream and our marriage started falling apart. I was overwhelmed by everything and started dating guys from the internet. When I first got married at the tender age of twenty-two, I was more the emotional age of a twelve year old. I had borderline personality disorder, my father had schizophrenia and now my first-born son Alex, was diagnosed with autism.

Welcome Austin

Alex got accepted to a special early intervention program at the Agassiz school in Jamaica Plain. Alex's teacher at this school was the mother of two of the children I had at the Small Fry preschool. I was her son Eddie's and daughter Carolyn's teacher and now she was my son's teacher! Alex got into a lot of trouble in her classroom, always shouting and running around. He got into fights with the other children. But his vocabulary greatly improved. And he started talking more.

My father simply adored Alex. He loved Austin too. But my dad always said that Alex was "a boy's boy". My father took Alex to the horse track. Alex used to call him Papa. Alex would get all excited when he saw the horses racing. He would jump up and down and say to my father "look Papa, a horse is running." My father would also let Alex scratch the lottery tickets with a penny. My father would get on the floor and play with Alex. He loved being a grandfather. It was harder for my father to interact with Austin, because Austin was still a baby. In fact Alex used to say himself all the time, "Austin's just a baby; Alex is a man."

Andrew got a new job at First Notice finally doing computer programming and making a higher salary. Andrew also got a vasectomy. Even though we wanted a daughter, we both thought that two children were enough. It was nice that the two boys were only two years apart. Alex started interacting a lot more with Austin. As an older brother he would often blame poor Austin for everything. Austin could barely crawl and didn't move much. Yet Alex would tell me "look mom, Austin made that mess", the glint of the devil in his eyes as he said it!

Both boys shared a bedroom. But Alex would often fall asleep on our bed or the living room floor. Andrew had to pick him up and put him back in his own bed. Alex called our bed "flower power". We had a green comforter with huge magnolia flowers all over it. He called his bed "the Mickey", because there were pictures of Mickey Mouse on his light blue comforter. So, every night he would say at bedtime "no Mickey, flower power and tv on". That's because we had a television in our room.

Alex developed asthma one winter. We thought he just had a cold. But he was struggling to breathe, and he was wheezing. When we took him to the pediatrician, they gave us a nebulizer to take home and a prescription for albuterol. The nebulizer is a machine that has a mask that you place over your face in which you breathe into. You fill it with the albuterol to clear up the passageways. Alex called this machine "his nebs" and was always eager to use it when he wasn't feeling very well.

One time his asthma got so bad that he needed to be hospitalized overnight. We all stayed in the same room with him, Andrew, me and even Austin in his little baby carrier. I didn't want to be separated from him, even for a night. He needed around the clock care. But by the next day he was doing well enough to go home. Thank God for that nebulizer. The insurance covered the cost.

Welcome Austin

My father was getting friendly with my on-line buddies. I was leading a double life. I was married with small children and seeing other men. Although at this time I wasn't having sex with any of these guys. It was more like what a teenager does, make-out and stuff like that. I never dated until I was almost nineteen. And then I married him. I never knew what it was like to be with another man. I went to an all-girl catholic high school. I never went to parties or the prom. I never even went to the senior banquet they had for us before graduation.

I was having a one-sided open marriage because Andrew knew what was going on. Yet Andrew never cheated on me. I was chewing my wild oats. Austin was too young yet to understand. But the tension in the house did affect Alex. When Andrew and I would fight Alex would scream at us both saying, "get out of my living room". It was as if Alex wanted us to go to our respected corners and cool down. Andrew was always a great husband and father. He didn't deserve my openly cheating on him. My father understood what I was going through because he himself went through it in his marriage. In fact, his whole family cheated on their spouses. It wasn't rare at all. My aunt Connie had two affairs, one lasting two years!

My marriage was starting to crumble apart. I had asked my parents if I could move into the downstairs apartment with them. My father said yes. But my mother vehemently refused. I wasn't working and I had two small kids, one with special needs. There was no place else I could go. Andrew could always move back with his parents in Walpole. But Andrew didn't want to leave his kids. We were really stuck.

Chapter 8

Pneumococcal Meningitis

It was Maundy Thursday. In three days it would be Easter Sunday. We had been getting ready preparing Easter baskets for the boys and going to the mall having their picture taken with the Easter bunny. Alex was feeling very sick. It appeared like he had a bad cold. Alex was always getting sick or coming down with ear infections. As a precaution Andrew took him to the pediatrician, while I stayed home with Austin. The pediatrician put him on an antibiotic.

We put Alex to bed early that night and he slept the whole night. When Andrew went in his room the next morning to check on him before he went to work, he called for me to come into Alex's room quickly. Alex wasn't responsive. He was stiff as a board, and his eyes were rolled back in his head. He immediately called 911and I explained the condition that our son was in. The person on the other end of the phone said that it sounded like meningitis.

We had 2 ambulances at our doorstep right away. They came into Alex's room and stabilized him enough to whisk him off to Children's hospital. My father came upstairs to see what all the commotion was about. The look on my father's face was one of shock and total devastation. How could this be happening? It was April 20, 2000. It was also Good Friday, although it was the worst day of our lives. When Alex left in that ambulance that day it was the last time, he would ever live at home with us again.

They kept Alex in insolation in the intensive care unit at Children's Hospital in Boston after running a battery of tests on him all morning. He was unconscious and in a coma. They did think he would wake from the coma, though. He was hooked up to all sorts of wires and machines. I felt completely numb to all of this. I don't think I could feel at all. I was in such complete and utter shock. There in the intensive care unit I saw a lot of other very sick children. One child with cancer needed a bone marrow transplant and was in agonizing pain. His mother was lying next to him on the bed when his father came in from out of town.

Of course, we had the difficult job of alerting every one of Alex's illness, both his school and our families. He woke up on Easter Sunday. But he didn't recognize us, and he was cross-eyed. He couldn't talk or even move. They had to feed him through IV's. It was clear that he had extensive brain damage from this. He could have died. The doctors couldn't promise us anything. They couldn't give us any answers. All they said was that the chance of an autistic child getting meningitis was less than the chance of getting struck by lightning. Alex was now having seizures and put on a cocktail of very heavy medicines that he would have to remain on for the rest of his life.

Alex spent two weeks at Children's hospital. He was transferred over to a room there that he shared with a teenage boy that had a brain tumor. There was suffering and pain all around. Alex had to learn everything all over again. His eyes went from deep blue to a slate grey. He couldn't sit up or feed himself and he had no speech. It was if he died and was reborn.

Pneumococcal Meningitis

Meningitis is an inflammation of the lining around the brain and spinal cord. Most severe cases are caused by bacteria. Pneumococcal meningitis occurs when the bacteria that have invaded the bloodstream move across to infect the 'meninges' (the membranes that surround and protect the brain and spinal cord). The meninges are filled with a liquid called cerebrospinal fluid (CSF), which is there to bathe the brain and cushion it against physical damage.

Bacteria can multiply freely in CSF, and there they release poisons, causing inflammation and swelling in the meninges and the brain tissue itself
As the disease progresses the patient becomes drowsy, confused, and delirious. They may have seizures and eventually lose consciousness. If inflammation and damage to the brain cannot be successfully stopped with antibiotics and other treatments, the infection can be fatal.

Usually the symptoms are a severe headache and stiff neck with extreme lethargy. Alex didn't display any of those symptoms the day before his coma when he was brought into the pediatrician's office. But meningitis can occur quite rapidly and without warning become fatal. Alex could have had these symptoms overnight, and then slipped into a coma the next morning. The terribly ironic and cruel thing is that the vaccination for meningitis came out only a few months AFTER Alex contacted it. I always made sure that both my sons were immunized as soon as the vaccines came out. They both were for the chicken pox. Austin immediately received the vaccine for meningitis as soon as it was available.

Life with My Schizophrenic Father

My father always came to visit Alex alone. My mother said she was always busy "doing her hair, or cooking. Alex's pediatrician from Newton Wellesley Hospital, who had a son named Alex herself, came to see him, and to personally offer us her support. Even his teacher from the Agazzi came to visit, and so did Andrew's brother, David. We had to investigate a rehabilitation hospital for Alex next. We had two choices; one was the Spaulding. The other one was Franciscans Children's Hospital in Brighten. We went with Franciscan's because it specialized in children. All the patients were young children.

Franciscan's Hospital was to be Alex's new home for the next two years. My marriage to Andrew was destroyed. I spent all day at the hospital with Alex and then had Randy (a man I was dating from the internet) pick me up at six-thirty every evening right from the hospital. I barely crossed paths with Andrew, who came every morning and then after work every evening as well. My parents took care of Austin during the days when I was at the hospital. Andrew put him to bed every evening when I was out with Randy.

Randy was ten years older than me and married himself. He also married his first girlfriend. He was the manager of Lowe's movie theater at that time. And he had two teenage daughters. He was not in love with his wife. He came to the hospital every Friday to personally visit Alex. Randy was the escape that I needed to get away from a life that was falling apart all around me.

Pneumococcal Meningitis

At Franciscan's, Alex shared a room with another boy named Alex, who had lived at the hospital since he was six months old. They both had a soma bed enclosed with netting that zipped all around the frame for protection. Alex had therapy around the clock, both physical therapy and speech therapy. And he was also seen by the staff psychologist Suzy. There were many doctors and nurses, as well as social workers we had to deal with that helped Alex.
I went to all of Alex's therapies with him all during the day. At the beginning he was very quiet.

During this time, I became very serious with Randy. He told his wife about me and asked her for a divorce. He moved out of the house that they were sharing with their children and into the in-law space his mother lived in, which was a private section of the house his brother David owned. David's wife and children lived in the other part of the house. And I saw them all the time when we used to go visit his mother.

I told my husband I wanted a divorce as well. I was very much a part of Randy's world. I had dinners with his family, including his daughters and niece. All his coworkers at the theater knew me. He was the very first man I had sex with besides my husband. We had this elaborate plan of leaving our spouses and marrying each other. We enjoyed the same things, golf, bowling and baseball. He even paid for me to have private golf lessons. And we were both very much crazy, unconventional people who did our own thing.

Life with My Schizophrenic Father

My parents got along with Randy well, especially my father. Randy and my father loved to talk sports, something my father could never do with Andrew. Both Randy and my father smoked. They were both a little crazy, well actually a lot crazy. I felt, like for once, that I fit in with Randy's family. I never felt that way with Andrew's family. It just seemed like I belonged. I especially liked his mother Ogenia.

At this point in my life everything was topsy-turvy. My world was upside/down. Nothing felt consistent or secure. Alex was making progress physically. But Alex had regressed tremendously emotionally and intellectually. He was now able to sit and eat on his own They removed his feeding tube. He still had very poor fine motor skills. But he learned how to walk again. He also started acting more like a wild, uncontrollable animal rather than a five-year-old boy. For this reason alone, they confided him to a wheelchair even though he could now walk on his own.

Brain damage can result in poor impulse control and aggression. And now that is what we were experiencing from Alex. When he would be wheeled down for speech therapy he would spit at the therapist. She would have to stop and have him wheeled back to his room. One time when I came to visit him, he had removed his diaper and smeared his shit all over the enclosed soma bed. It was a horrible sight to see. The room reeked of the smell of his shit and the bed was a total mess. He was covered in his own excrement. It even looked like he was feasting on it.

Pneumococcal Meningitis

Alex was getting to be too much of a handful for the hospital to handle. They said after a few months that they have done everything that they could do for him. The social worker called me up and asked if I wanted to bring the soma bed home with me. She said it was time for Alex to move back home. I was very hesitant. Alex needed around the clock care. I certainly couldn't keep him in a soma bed all day. I tried to get in touch with the Boston Public School system, but it was the summer, and everything was closed.

There was nowhere to turn to for help. So, I wrote the superintendent of the Boston Public Schools Thomas Payzant and told him that the law should be changed to help children that are in need during the summer. He did do something about it. After I told him my story about Alex, he changed that law. But it was too late to help my son Alex. I would have to wait until the fall when the school system resumed their sessions.

But when the fall arrived Boston didn't want to help Alex at all. They wouldn't take him back because he was severely brain damaged and he couldn't stay in the hospital because he was physically healthy. So, the social worker suggested I contact a lawyer. There were special places/homes for children with handicaps so severe such as Alex's, but they were quite expensive. Who would pay for it? Boston Public School's was responsible for his education. But they refused to budge.

I obtained a State Street lawyer named Peter Gossels and sued the Boston Public School system for not supporting Alex because of his handicap. The money that Andrew had saved up to help pay for the divorce was put as a down payment to obtain this very expensive lawyer. The divorce was off for now. We had a much bigger fight on our hands
And it would take years to finally resolve it. The hospital knew what we were up against. So Franciscan's agreed to be Alex's temporary home until we found him a new one.

This was going to be the biggest battle of our lives. We were going up against the Boston Public School system. We had a major legal war on our hands. Meanwhile, Alex was starting to deteriorate at the hospital because he was kept in a wheelchair all day. He was always assigned a one-on-one person to keep a watch on him . But even Alex outsmarted each person he was assigned to.

Alex was in the wheelchair for his own protection because he was very aggressive and fast moving and had no safety awareness due to his extensive brain damage.
One time his personal staff took him for a walk in his wheelchair. The staff he was with turned their back for a split second and Alex took off. He got on the elevator himself and kept pressing all the buttons. It was total mayhem. When I got there, it sounded like a page from that children's book about the little monkey who always got into trouble, the one "Curious George Goes
to the Hospital".

Pneumococcal Meningitis

The tension between Andrew and I was so thick that you could cut it with a knife. It all began when I borrowed a sundress from my mother without asking her. She was angry and yelling at me. And then Andrew started yelling at me. We got into a fight. I became frightened and called the police. I told them that Andrew was beating me, which wasn't true. At the time I think I was delusional. I certainly was in a psychotic "borderline state" where reality became blurred. I just snapped under the pressure and so did Andrew.

The police came to our house and took Andrew away in handcuffs. I immediately called Randy and told him what had happed and that I was frightened. As soon as he got to my house, I told him that I wanted to go to the police station and get Andrew out. I wanted to tell them that it was all a big, bad mistake. So, Randy drove me down there. I talked to the sergeant. He told me there was a restraining order on Andrew and that he had to stay away from our house. So, for a week Andrew moved in with his parents until we were able to lift the restraining order. During that week Randy lived with me at my house. But this was the beginning of the end for Randy and me.

The next day when I walked into the hospital Alex had a meltdown and threw a very heavy toy at my face that almost gorged my eye. I had to put ice on it right away. I was headed for a nervous breakdown. Currently, I wasn't receiving professional help. I would later make up for all the years that I need psychological help by going to many different psychologists for the rest of my life.

The court dropped the restraining order and Andrew was able to move back home on the condition that we go for marriage counseling for a minimum of one year. We found a counseling center in Needham. We had a middle-aged therapist named Beth who I thought was kind but not too bright. We went there once a week and then went to the local Chinese restaurant for dinner afterwards.

Once Randy got word of this, he broke off with me. I think he wanted to "bow out gracefully" and allow me to work on my marriage, either that or he become very frightened of the state I was in, which wasn't very pretty. I didn't take it too hard. It was a minor thing compared to everything else that was going on at the time. I think his mother had a lot of influence in his decision, though. Being a good catholic girl, I went to confession and confessed my sins openly (face to face) with the priest. Randy and I are still friends to this day.

Chapter 9

The Wyllie's vs. the Boston Public School System

The Boston Public school system was going to slowly drag their feet for as long as it could so as not to pay for Alex's care. But it was quite evident that Alex needed constant around the clock care. Meanwhile, Mark a school liaison that worked at Franciscan was searching for specialized places for Alex. And some of those places were out of state.
We had to accept whatever was available. We even checked out the Boston Higashi School in Randolph, the school specialized in helping children with autism. But although Alex was diagnosed originally with autism his brain injury was what was impairing him now, not his autism.

We spent an afternoon at Higashi and we took Alex with us. We even dressed up in kimonos. We toured the facility. They had miniature sinks and toilets in their bathrooms, just the right size for small children. There was only one caveat; they closed the whole month of August. What would we do for that month? We couldn't take Alex home. He was very aggressive because of his brain injury and getting bigger by the day. Often times he would try to choke me, and he would hurl anything that he could get his hands on as a weapon. He was still in diapers, had no language or receptive understanding of anything. So because of that we nixed the idea of the Higashi School.

My father would visit Alex faithfully every Sunday. Of course, my mother never came. We would get a pass to take Alex out to Duncan Donuts for a chocolate covered donut and an ice-coffee. We weren't supposed to give Alex caffeine or sugar, but it was only once a week and he loved it so much. Andrew's parents did visit him once at his fifth birthday party held at the hospital in the children's playroom.

Life with My Schizophrenic Father

My father drove me to the hospital every morning to see Alex during the weekdays. He was very good with Alex. He didn't treat him any differently than he did before. Andrew visited Alex every morning before going off to work. He would feed Alex his breakfast. That would be their special time together. Alex usually ate yogurt in the morning. Alex would spend a lot of time in his room zipped up in the netted soma bed watching Nickelodeon. He especially liked Blue's Clues. Before his illness he loved Thomas the Tank Engine. We had so many Thomas wooden trains and tracks in our house. He could build a track across two rooms! He would spend hours doing this. He also used to love to draw. He would draw pictures of his bedroom. I still have those pictures. Now he couldn't even hold a crayon in his hand.

I would take him for walks outside the hospital on good days. The hospital became like a second home to us. I was there seven days a week. I had no life that existed outside of it now that Randy was gone. I was extremely isolated and alone. I had no friends.

I did attend a parent's support group at this time that was held at the hospital. I listened to other mother's whose children were residents at the hospital just like Alex. It was heartbreaking to hear some of these women. One in particular I remember. I went to visit her one-year old baby, who was hanging on by a thread. I'll never forget seeing her little one hooked up to ever gizmo available to keep his fragile body alive. He wasn't even supposed to be born alive, let alone live for a year. The doctors told her to abort the pregnancy. But she held on. I'll never forget the chill I had down my spine when I saw the ambulance take him away for the very last time. She had fought the fight for so long and lost.

The Wyllie's vs. the Boston Public School System

I saw a lot of children in far worse shape than Alex at Franciscan. There was this little oriental boy named Leo. He had almost died from drowning. He had severe brain damage from the incident that should have taken his life. The severity of the brain damage affects patients differently. All Leo could do was blink his eyes. He had no movement at all. And there was no optimistic prognosis for him either. He could breathe on his own, but aside from that and blinking his eyes there was not much else that poor little boy could do except lay in bed all day, a prisoner in his own body.

There was another female patient named Shanelle. She was a black teenage girl. All she would do is scream every day. When she wasn't in bed she was confined to a wheelchair like Alex. I never noticed anyone ever come to visit her. At least Leo's parents always came to see him. On Father's Day Andrew told me a nurse said to him "two". He asked the nurse what she meant by saying that number. Her answer was that Andrew and Leo's father were the ONLY father's that showed up at the hospital to visit their children on Father's Day. What a pity. Some of these kids were left sick and on their own at the hospital. Some families just abandoned their kids. They could not cope. What a tragedy.

We had our plates filled but we religiously went to see Alex EVERY day of the week, including holidays. We had Thanksgiving and Christmas at that hospital for two years. It just became a way of life that we had to adapt to. There was never a question of would we or could we do it.

We kept looking into different places to put Alex. There was another boy at the hospital name Albert (Berto for short). His mother allowed him to play out in the street late at night without supervision. He came from a very large Spanish family. It was ten o'clock at night when he was struck by a bus, much too late for a small boy to be playing in the street without supervision. He was playing "chicken" with a bus and the bus won. He got ran over by that bus which landed him at Franciscan. He was a very boisterous child that always commanded attention from the staff, and really anyone else that crossed his path. He had red curly hair and big, brown doe eyes. And he flirted with every lady, no matter what age they were.

The May Center was a residential home that catered to brain damaged children. They were coming up to look at Berto. We thought maybe the May Center might have a look at Alex while they were up. But we still had to get Boston to foot the bill.

Dr. Wilson had a talk with someone from the Boston Public Schools and told them directly that Alex was deteriorating from lying around the hospital all day and not getting the proper help that he needed. He said that there was only a small "window of opportunity" for Alex and that it was slowly closing. Dr. Wilson also said that he would testify in court and give his medical opinion of what was happening to Alex by Boston "holding out" on him. This was the match that lit the fire under their ass to finally act, because God knows our lawyer wasn't really doing anything except milking us of our money.

The Wyllie's vs. the Boston Public School System

Somehow Dr. Wilson must have stepped on the right toes because shortly after that Boston suddenly agreed that Alex did indeed need a residential place and that they would pay for it until Alex reached the age of twenty-two. So, the May Center that took Berto came to look at Alex. But unfortunately, they did not have a bed for him. What they did have is a spot in the Arlington program during the days. Everyone agreed that Alex would be transported To the Arlington May Center during the day and back to Franciscan at night until a bed opened up for him somewhere in the May program.

Alex did exceptionally well at the May in Arlington. He began to acquire some language. He started calling us mom and dad again and using a handful of words. It was so good to finally hear him call us by name and recognize that we were his parents. It was music to our ears. I was worried that he would never be able to speak again and that I would never be able to communicate with him. They also were teaching him the alphabet and numbers and fine motor skills like zippering and buttoning.

Meanwhile Andrew and I were checking out residences at different May locations that Alex might be able to attend. There was a place on the cape they thought might have an opening. It was in Chatham. It was a lovely residence very close to the water. But it was also a two-hour drive one way. We thought that if he lived there, we would have to spend an overnight on the cape every weekend just to see our son. But considering that some places we were looking into were as far away as Virginia we were at least content to know that this was doable.

Life with My Schizophrenic Father

We were all set to accept Chatham when another opening at a residential home in the May became available that was much closer to us. In fact, it was right over the town line of Randolph, only minutes from the Higashi School that we once visited. The house was on Lakeview Ave. in Holbrook. It was only about a forty-minute drive away. It was a residential place for small boys. Alex was six at the time. And that was the starting age for this house. The director gave us a tour and we were impressed. It was a huge house. There were four bedrooms upstairs. Alex would share a bedroom with another boy. They had two living rooms, a dining room. The yard was big and enclosed. And it was in a very nice rural neighborhood. Across the street was a huge lake that sat on several people's properties, hence "Lakeview".

The school that he would be attending would be in Brocton. He would be escorted from the residence by a van to the school every day. Holbrook would also have staff take him to our house for visits. They would stay with him during the visits as well. It would be something to think about since Alex had never been home since before his illness. This would be a brand-new beginning for Alex, and even for us.

Alex's home for the last two years was at Franciscan's. It's a small hospital with only seventy-two beds. The nurses got to know Alex personally and became attached to him, as well as the one-on–one person he had assigned for him during the day. One nurse said she could always get Alex to smile by nuzzling her nose in his ear. It was an intimate setting, unlike the larger sterile hospitals. And in a way, it had become my home too. Although I was only too happy to get Alex out of the hospital at last, I was certainly going to miss this place.

The Wyllie's vs. the Boston Public School System

We had one special night out before Alex left the hospital for good. We received tickets through the hospital to see Disney on Ice do the musical "Toy Story". It was playing in Boston at the Garden. I asked my father if he would take us. He agreed and we all went together. My father was a natural with Alex. Andrew never took Alex out of the hospital. He was too afraid that Alex would act up in public and that we wouldn't be able to control him. But my father never worried about anything like that. He treated Alex as he had always done prior to the meningitis.

We enjoyed a good evening at the ice show. Alex really was smiling broadly with wide-eyed amazement as the characters came to life on the rink. Because of the brain damage Alex can tend to have a very short attention span and get distracted easily. But this evening he sat quietly and was fully immersed in the silly antics of Woody and his gang. My dad got Alex popcorn and we took pictures with the characters.

When my dad took Alex back to the hospital, he was very tired from a much enjoyed evening out. It was also late at night too, well past his bedtime. This was one of those very special moments I will never forget of the three of us. And it was one of the last fond memories I would have of Alex and my father. My father would sadly never get to visit Alex when he went to live at the May Center.

Austin had been accustomed to Franciscan as well, not only by attending the day program there but also by visiting Alex on a regular basis. There was a private playroom they allowed us to use with Alex. It was very small. The hospital psychologist Suzy had sessions in there when she was not using her main office. The hospital also had a much larger playroom on Alex's floor that had many toys, books and puzzles. That was open for all the children to use. There were events held in there as well as arts and crafts, and group activities such as Bingo and playing board games. One of the staff was in charge of directing all of the activities. They also had cooking classes as well for the children. But Alex never attended those.

In this private playroom Austin and Alex got to interact with each other. There were no words between them, but you could see the glow of love on their faces. One time when they were playing around, they held each other close and stared with brotherly love deeply into each other's eyes. I was lucky enough to capture that moment on a picture. That year I made copies of the picture and sent it out to everyone as a Christmas card greeting. The people who received it thought Alex had gotten all better. In that picture you could never tell that Alex was brain damaged. He was looking deeply into Austin's eyes with recognition and love.

Alex knew who his brother was, even if he forgot everything else. He knew and loved Austin. There was a very large outdoor playground right at the hospital. We would take both boys out there in the warm weather. One time when Austin fell off the slide Alex came rushing over to his aid. He didn't have any language then but you could see the concerned look on his face that he had for Austin. He wanted to make sure that his brother was alright.

Chapter 10

The May Center

The last day at the hospital was like any other day for Alex. He didn't know it was going to be his last and that he would have a brand-new place to live with all new people to get to know. It was a bright, sunny, warm spring day in May. The year was 2002. He was wheeled out by his one-on-one guy named Del, whose brother Kim also was a one-on-one to Ale as well. He was put on a van and sent to Holbrook.

When he got to the residential house he ran up and down the stairs yelling "mom" and "dad". He couldn't understand why we weren't there. We always had visited him when he was at Franciscan's every day. Things would be different now. We could not see him every day because it would interfere with his routine. We would be allowed some planned visits, but it wouldn't be like it was at the hospital. The May Center would teach Alex many things, like how to go the bathroom on his own, how to eat on his own, and how to dress on his own. The school would teach him simple math and English.

He had a chart with pictured words at first. So, the way he was taught to communicate was to point to the words as he learned them. This chart had words with pictures under each one of them for all his needs like "bathroom", "food", and different activities that Alex would like to do. He earned chocolate candy if he obeyed and followed directions. It was a completely different way of life than just sitting around the hospital all day in a wheelchair. Here, Alex got to be a real boy. He never saw that wheelchair or enclosed soma bed again!

Life with My Schizophrenic Father

We set up a plan of coming to see Alex twice during the week and once on the weekends. We always brought Austin with us when we went so that Alex wouldn't forget that he had a brother. Austin became the little brother to all the other boys at the house as well. The other boys were older than Alex. And they all had different issues that brought them there. Some could talk very well, and others couldn't. Some of them had a lot of emotional issues like Alex. One boy liked to draw and would always show me his artwork. The May took the boys out to movies and the lake, hiking and bowling. They lived like regular kids. Alex got to go to the YMCA every week, which he loved. They had a big slide that went right into the pool.

We celebrated the holidays at the May as well. We took Alex trick-or-treating on Halloween. We had a big turkey dinner with all the trimmings that one of the staff prepared and served to us on Thanksgiving Day. The same was true at Christmas as well. We took Alex for walks around the neighborhood. They had field trips out to places like the zoo. We joined them one time when he went to the Franklin Park Zoo. We took Austin with us as well. There was always plenty of staff around to help out if Alex had a melt-down.

We also met for bi-annual meetings at Alex's school in Brocton. The building used to be a nursing home that got converted over to become a school for the May Center. A liaison from the Boston Public School's would be present at these meetings, along with Alex's teacher and nurse and therapy workers from the school, as well as the staff at the residence. He was assigned a case worker at the residence that kept track of everything. Each person would take their turn talking about Alex's progress. And we made up goals for the next six-months for him.

The May Center

The first time we took Alex back to our house it was a disaster. Staff drove Alex back to his old home. He hadn't been home in over two years. The staff stayed there with him. Alex ran amok in and out of every room. He threw things and knocked over lamps. He did however; look at the many pictures that were on the walls. Maybe there was some recognition there. He went in his own bedroom and jumped on his bed. I don't know if there was any awareness or if he had any memory of his bedroom before his illness. But he was becoming very destructive, so it was a very short visit and the staff drove him back early to the May Center.

My parents did not see him. We thought it would be too overwhelming for Alex on his very first visit home. I think just the initial visit to the upstairs apartment where he used to live would be enough for him to take in. It was kind of a disappointment that the visit didn't go well. But Alex would do better slowly over time on these visits home, which would occur every Sunday. We would eventually be able to have him stay for dinner with a staff member assigned to him.

Alex still had seizures although he was put on Kepra, and Tegretol. His seizures would scare me. It was like he was in a trance. He stared wide eyed in a daze and was unresponsive except for involuntary movements of his hands and fingers sometimes. It was very important to time each seizure. Sometimes they would need to adjust the dosage of the medication to make sure he was at the right level.

Alex also suffered pica and severe acid reflux from regurgitating his food. Pica is a tendency or craving to eat substances other than normal food, like clay, plaster or any other small objects. So we needed to be real careful what Alex would put in his mouth. The regurgitation was pretty bad too, because he would bring up the acid in his stomach. There were just so many issues with Alex's health all the time. He was sent to specialists, a neurologist and an immunologist. They discovered something new about Alex. He had a compromised immune system. This is probably the reason why he contacted meningitis in the first place. Alex was put on daily antibiotics as well to prevent him from getting infections.

Alex was sicker than we realized, even prior to his meningitis. We never even knew he had an immune deficiency. We always brought him to the pediatrician. He never missed a visit. And he received all his vaccinations on schedule. He was growing well as a child. In fact he was in the 90th percentile for height and weight on his charts. He was breast-fed for two years. We fed him very well, although he was an extremely fussy eater. We did all we could do. It is one of those things in life that has no explanation. When we were at Children's Hospital, we saw little babies dying of cancer. We saw children suffering every day in great pain. There are no answers for any of this. It is all an unfortunate part of life. It is a heartbreaking reality that we must live with each and every day for the rest of our lives.

The May Center

My father was not doing well currently either. I heard stories that he was going after my mother with a knife. I've never known my father to be a violent man, but he wasn't taking his medication. And I know just how bad my father gets when he goes off his medicine. I was involved in my own personal hell with my son, so I kept out of it. My mother called the police on him. I'm not quite sure what happened after that. But I did notice him standing outside on a very cold winter's day in just his underwear. He looked like a homeless man.

During this time we decided to go back to church. We needed something to cling to for our sanity. There was a new minister there named Weldon Palmer. His daughter Franny had a brain tumor and was admitted to Franciscan's Children's Hospital. Andrew thought that he should call him because he clearly understood what he was going through, since not that long-ago Alex was staying there. That one phone call where Andrew reached out to him as a father who also had a very sick child, and not just another parishioner in need meant the world to Weldon. It is something he never forgot. And as a result, we both got quite close to him.

I confided a lot to Weldon. I told him about my affair with Randy. I told him about how sick my father was as well. At this time Andrew got fired from his job at First Notice and we were on unemployment. Weldon helped pay some of our bills with his minister's fund. He was an incredibly generous and kind man. Unfortunately, many people at our church did not think so.

Life with My Schizophrenic Father

There was a group of people, almost half the church that did not like Weldon and wanted him thrown out. The church was completely divided over him. Some people left the church and others became estranged from certain members deciding on what side of the fence they were on. We tried our very best to rally for Weldon. We attended meetings and wrote living testimonies about how much he had helped us. Weldon not only paid for some of our bills but he also got us professional help. He introduced us to Dr. Alan O'Hare, who was his very good friend. Alan gave us marriage counseling for free. He was located in Sharon. Weldon also set me up with another psychologist, Dr. Beth Freed in Norwood so I could have individual therapy as well.

I never went to a psychologist before. My mother was dead set against them. My father had been seeing Dr. Robert Torchin, but he was a psychiatrist that only prescribed medication for him. My father didn't really do therapy with him. I was very grateful for this help, especially Alan, Weldon's friend. He was a very tall man, over six for five. He had medium gray, wavy hair. And he also sported a mustache. He looked like a nature guy in his sandals and jeans. On the very first session he asked us both "what do you need; what do you want?" Andrew started seeing his own psychologist too at the therapy center right next to the church. Alan used to be the head of that center but had recently retired. Alan was also involved with the theater and storytelling.

The May Center

The church finally threatened Weldon so much that he had to finally resign. We were devastated. The associate pastor Nan, a very bubbly, robust and gregarious woman also gave her resignation along with him. Although no one had any problems with her staying she just couldn't in good faith continue on without her very dear friend Weldon by her side. This was another major loss in my life. The next time I would see Weldon again would be at my mother's funeral. His parting words to me were "I love you and your family."

We stopped going to church. We felt very isolated until one warm, sunny Saturday evening in spring. We had just finished dinner at Bertuccci's, our usual haunt for Italian food. It was too nice out to go back home so we took Austin to the local park across the street from the restaurant. I wanted to walk some laps around the park to work off the big Italian dinner I had just eaten. So, Andrew sat on the bench and stayed with Austin. Austin discovered another boy there his age named Michael. And the two of them started playing together in the sand. Michael's mother struck up a conversation with Andrew. She told him that her other son was at Brigham and Woman's Hospital. He was born very prematurely. She wanted to take Michael to a park close by because they were just coming back from the hospital visiting him.
When I finished my laps, I saw her talking to Andrew and stopped to introduce myself. That was the beginning of a very endearing friendship.

Her name was Holly. I told her about my other son Alex and that he was at the May Center and his history. Her son Michael was autistic too. She was also Italian, and her birthday was exactly one day before mine. She was born July 10, 1965 and I was born July 11, 1965. We had so much in common and our sons were enjoying playing together so much that I invited her and her husband and son Michael over for lunch. And the friendship took off from there. Ironically it was that same park I met my friend Linda at too.

The therapy with Dr. Freed was not going well. She really wasn't helping me at all. So, I left her a message on her answering machine that I wasn't going to continue therapy with her anymore. I never heard back from her upon leaving her that message and I never saw her again. It really is a shame that I ended therapy because what would happen next would be a triple tragedy of mammoth proportions.

My father was now committed to McLean Hospital. He was also dying of cancer. We didn't know this at the time he was at McLean. The nurses thought he wasn't eating because he thought that the food was poisoned. I brought in home cooked food for him to eat at the hospital, but he refused everything. The real reason he couldn't eat was because he was in terrible pain from the cancer that racked his body. He had a very large tumor on his liver. But no one knew this at the time.

Chapter 11

Back To Back Death of My Parents

Alex was at the May and my dad was at Mclean. It was quite a juggle having two sick people that I loved in my life and visiting them both all the time. And then the Saturday after Thanking when we came home from shopping, we noticed an ambulance outside our house and paramedics going inside my parent's house. All the neighbors were standing on the sidewalk in front of our house as well. My aunt Connie was over and my cousin Steven as well. They told me that my mother had died unexpectedly of heart failure. Although I had no real love for my mother I was devastated because my father was in the hospital, and I'm not sure they would allow him out for her funeral.

My father had no idea that my mother was even sick. My cousin Steven swooped in like a knight in shining armor and said that he would take care of everything, since I was an only child. I always loved Steven and looked up to him as a big brother, since he lived in this same house as me years earlier. I would have the onerous job of going to McLean's and telling my father that his wife had passed away since he had been admitted. When I got to the hospital, I didn't know of any way to say it except straight out. He was in total shock. He broke down and cried. He said, "she didn't deserve it." She had died all alone in the house the day after Thanksgiving. I did not see her on Thanksgiving. I was having the holiday with my son, Alex at the May Center.

Steven helped me with all the funeral arrangements and the bills. He also helped my father pay his bills, or so we thought. We allowed him access to a lot of money. My father said that he loved him as if he was his own son. My parents had a bank account worth one hundred grand that I could use as part of their estate. I needed to get a lawyer to help me sort this out. McLean allowed my father a weekend pass.

We took my father out to dinner at Bertucci's, along with Austin. He could barely touch the food on his plate. He did try to eat, but every time he did he clutched his stomach in agonizing pain. I knew for certain that night that he couldn't eat because of the cancer. The same exact thing happened to my grandmother when she had colon cancer, because of the size of the tumor that was pressing on her stomach. This made it impossible to eat. It appeared that my father had colon cancer too that had spread to his liver.

We called that night "the last supper" because it was the last meal that we shared with my father. And since it was at Bertucci's every time we get that same exact table that my father and us sat that very same night of his last meal, we call that table "the last supper table". I don't like to be seated there, even now all these years later. The memory is as vivid as if it were yesterday. Of course, my father tried to kid not only himself but us by calling his pain indigestion. But I knew.

Back To Back Death Of My Parents

After that night I called McLean Hospital and tried to explain to the nurse the kind of pain my father was in from eating and that it had nothing to do with his paranoid delusions that the food was poisoned. I explained that his mother had these exact symptoms and that she had colon cancer. Of course, the nurse made me furious when she refused to listen to me.

My father looked very frail, since he had lost a lot of weight at McLean. On the day of my mother's funeral there were hardly any people there. I guess she didn't have many friends. Her best friend Sherry was in Florida at the time. I don't know where her other friend Sally was. My father's family was there, but there weren't that many people left on his side. I would say no more than a couple of dozen people were there at best. My father, despite his frail state stood up and told jokes. Everyone was laughing. It was like he was doing a comedy routine.

I was in for quite a surprise when my minister Weldon and his associate Nan came to visit me at the funeral home. I never thought I would see them again. They both sat next to me. They were my anchors. They were going through their own private hell with the church.
The real tragedy would be that in less than three months my father would return to this same funeral home, except this time he would be the one laid out in the casket.

That night I didn't sleep at all. If you don't believe in ghosts you will now when I tell you that my mother's spirit came to visit my house one last time. There was a picture of my two sons hanging on the wall. It came crashing down in the middle of the night for no reason at all. Pictures have never fallen off the walls in our house before. The next day we found a very large sum of money in my parent's living room hidden in the fireplace with a note from my mother. It had said that the money was for Austin's college fund. When I found it was the very first and the very last time I cried over my mother. The picture that came crashing down was an omen.

Steven was taking a lot of money from both my father and me to help pay our bills He was trying to negotiate with all the creditor we owed. I was still in shock. My father was no sooner released from McLean before he was admitted to the Faulkner hospital. There the doctors told me he had only a couple of months to live. I told the doctors that I would be the one to give the news to my father. So, after a couple of months of finding out his wife had died and burying her he was now faced with his own death staring him smack in the face.

When they released my father from the Faulkner to go back home to die, he didn't understand why none of his bills were paid when he was in the hospital. He gave everything over to Steven. I had to contend with my sick son Alex, the death of my mother and her funeral arrangements and my dying father all at once. Steven agreed to help out and was trusted with a large sum of money. It turned out that he had gambled all of my father's and my money away. Now I would have to get a lawyer to get my money back. He stole from my father and me when my father was dying. He took advantage of us when we were at our weakest, his own family. It was the start of yet another nightmare.

Back To Back Death of My Parents

I went to the police station and told the police. There was a warrant out for Steven's arrest. Apparently, Steven had stolen great sums of money from other people as well. My father died shortly after this, knowing that Steven had betrayed him. He had shut-off notices from every utility because Steven never paid the bills that he was supposed to while my father was in McLean Hospital.

My father and I shared a last lunch right before he died. He bought the most expensive cold-cuts and cheeses and fresh Italian bread. I really enjoyed his company, the conversation and the delicious food. He was prepared. He told me that he will be "leaving the earth". And he did shortly after that.

He wanted to be alone at the time of his death. I knew the day had come when I went down to visit him and he never answered the loud knocks on the door. The police came and knocked it down. He was found dead on the kitchen floor. It was February 19, 2004. I loved my father immensely. The one very ironic thing about it is my father made a killing at the casinos before he died. I found ten grand in cash in his pants pocket. He paid for his own funeral with this money.

I got food poisoning from eating sushi just days after his death. It wasn't a very good time for me to get sick. I still had to make all the arrangements and let people know. My father's half-brother Philly was livid at me. His son Steven was arrested the morning of my father's funeral. He gave me scathing looks the whole day of my father's funeral. Then my cousin Johnny took me aside to ask me what really happened with Steven. Steven had lied and made up stories and told them to everyone in the family.

My Father, Anthony Angelo Palladino,
as an MP during the Korean War

My parents and my father's parents, Sophie and Angelo
Palladino on my parent's wedding day in my aunt's basement,
September 2, 1962

Me at 2 years old - 1967

Me and my Dad around my third birthday

My bedroom in my parent's home The painting behind me done
by my Aunt Irene who was local artist in Quincy

My husband, Andrew, and I at his parent's home at Christmas 1986

New Year Eve '86. My parent's house

Dancing with my father on my wedding day,
September 12, 1987. My new husband, Andrew
is in the background dancing with my mother.

On my wedding day - my father's family starting from left:
Half-brother Philly, half-sister Rosie, my mother, Edith,
Andrew, me, my dad, his half-sister Edith, half-sister Mary, his
mother Sophie, and his half-sister Connie

Our oldest son, Alex, Age 11 months with a favorite
Teddy bear

Alex and Austin playing in the backyard - Early 2000

At the zoo, spring 2000

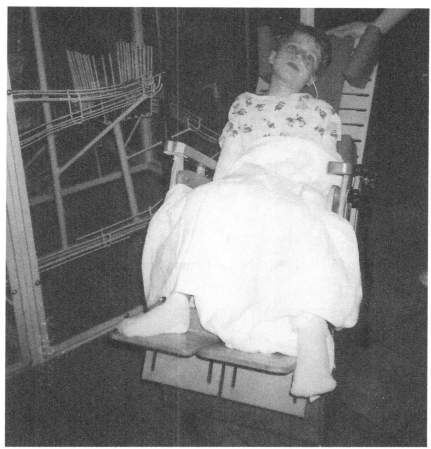

Alex during his two week stay at Children's Hospital Boston after contracting meningitis. April 2000.Wheelchair is reclined since he could not sit up on his own.

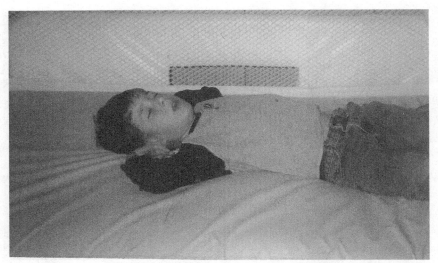

Alex asleep in his SOMA bed at Franciscan Childrens Hospital

Visiting Boston Hagashi School for their Bon Dance

Andrew with Alex at Franciscan's - Christmas 2001

Alex and Austin in one of the small playrooms at Franciscans
.April 2001

Alex with Andrew's parents, Bunny and Bruce Wyllie, at
Franciscans Hospital – August 2001

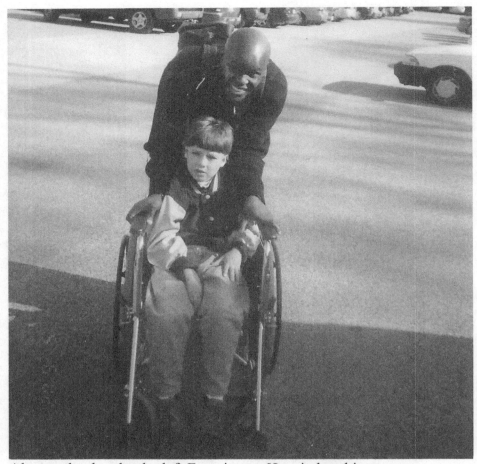

Alex on the day that he left Franciscans Hospital on his way to
the May Institute - May 6, 2002

Austin, myself & Alex at the Holbrooke Residence of the May Center

Alex's 9th Birthday at the May Center Residence

Halloween at the May – 2004

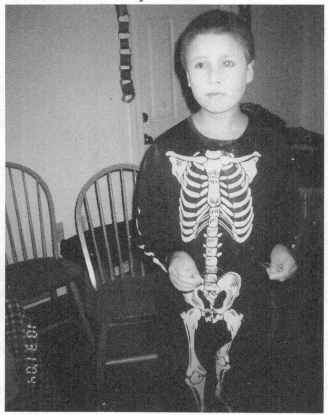

Last picture of Alex with my Dad

Alex today

Life with My Schizophrenic Father

The day of my father's funeral they had the military acknowledge my father with a large American flag and salute. They folded the flag in a triangle and handed it over to me in his honor. I put it on display in my dining room cabinet behind the glass.

Austin started martial art classes in West Roxbury that same day as well. We came straight from the reception immediately following and took him to the class. I was still all dressed in black. I didn't think that Austin should miss his very first class. I was still in a deep state of shock from burying both of my parents in a matter of less than three months apart from each other. And the lawsuit with my cousin was still ensuing. I was suing him for $35,000 of the money he took from my inheritance.

At the same time, I wanted to sell the two family home that I grew up in. I had nothing but very tragic memories in that house. Both of my parents died in that house, my mother in the living room and my father in the kitchen. And my son was stricken with the deadly disease of meningitis, in his own bedroom Easter weekend of 2000. I wanted out of that place as soon as possible. I contacted the real estate agent that had an office next door to my house. They told me to list it at 465,000. I thought that was low. But they said that it would sit for months on the market if I put the price up any higher.

So now we had the undaunted task of house hunting. I wanted a small, single family home. I lived in a two family all of my life. I always had someone living upstairs or downstairs from me. I wanted my own private backyard with a nice deck.

Back To Back Death of My Parents

I finally got to meet Dr. Torchin, my father's psychiatrist, after all of those years. I called him up for an appointment. I told him that my father had passed away. He remembered my father very fondly. He was an older man who had a big house on a hill in Newton that had a very large in-ground pool. He saw his patients at his residence. He was very stern, with grey hair and glasses, accompanied by a notebook. He took copious notes during our session. I felt out of sorts with him. I asked him questions about my father. He said that my father felt like the black sheep of the family.

It was tough being an orphan at only thirty-eight years old, and an only child as well. My son would grow up as an only child too, even though technically he wasn't. His brother lived in another house and Alex couldn't really interact with him. I tried to compensate by becoming more like a sister to Austin. But Austin caught onto this and was upset that he didn't have a sibling close to his age to really play with. They could have been very best friends. They were only two years apart in age. But it was never to be.

I decided to look elsewhere for another therapist because it was clear that I just wanted Dr. Torchin because he reminded me of my father, who I missed so terribly.
It was all so surreal how everything happened to Alex and my parents and the battle with my cousin. I needed someone to talk to about all of this. I knew that I needed to get professional help.

Chapter 12

2005, A Transformative Year

After a long run of heartache, 2005 proved to be a transformative year. I won the lawsuit against my cousin and the judge demanded that he make full payment of the thirty-five grand he stole of my inheritance. Because of his financial situation (at that time) he was allowed to make these payments in installments over a year. Ironically this was a tiny little blip for him. He would soon become a millionaire operating one of the largest Ponzi schemes on record.

My house sold in just one week. I put it on the market for four hundred and sixty-five thousand dollars and was offered ten grand more. We immediately turned around and paid cash for a six-room ranch that was on a dead-end street just a couple of blocks from the house I grew up in. And then I met the most incredible person of a lifetime in the form of a psychologist named Dick. He was completely unorthodox. I fell madly in love with him at first sight. I saw him for five hours a week. He did all my therapy for free. Insurance only covers a limited amount of sessions per year. It was during this time that I felt a part of myself really emerge. He was a much older man, twenty-two years older than me. My father had recently died, and I was looking for a father figure. With Dick I finally found the freedom to express myself. I stripped completely naked for him during one of my sessions. He later wrote a paper about it. I wanted to have sex with him in the worse way. But although Dick was unorthodox, he was never unethical. It is always unethical for a psychologist to have any sexual contact with a patient.

Life with My Schizophrenic Father

I took up driving again. Most of my life I never drove. Andrew drove me anywhere I needed to be. I was very timid about driving. And both of my parents discouraged me from getting behind the wheel. It all started when I received a hundred-dollar ticket from a very large and intimidating officer for not pulling over when he was flashing his lights. I was not speeding. I was making a left-hand turn into my driveway. But as soon as a police or ambulance flashes their lights you are always supposed to pull over to allow them access to pass. I didn't do this. The cop told me sternly as he made out the ticket "you shouldn't be on the road if you don't know how to drive."

I never drove after that incident again until I became Dick's patient. Any time I even thought of driving my father would tell me that I was crazy and that the cops would be out there just waiting for me. I still fear cops today because of that incident. It was out of necessity in order to see Dick that I needed to get back on the road. My mother never drove either. My father would drive her everywhere. But it was different for me because I at least had my license. As I became more confident, I started driving to other local places. Dick gave me that confidence and security that had been lacking in me for so long.

2005, A Transformative Year

My borderline personality disorder really came out in the therapy with Dick. I was always "running away" from therapy. Sometimes his care seemed "over the top". My father was very caring and loving but his care was unpredictable and never stable. Because of his schizophrenia when he was delusional, he was in a different world, a world where no one could ever reach him. Dick had a lot of traits like my father. He was patient and kind and listened very attentively. But he was also different than my father in the way that he would hug me and always be a stable, reassuring presence in my life. Borderlines want and need to be loved, but they also feel that they don't deserve to be loved, so when they receive it they push it away.

I was always testing Dick to see if he really loved me. It wasn't enough that he gave me five hours of therapy every week for absolutely free. I would call him in the middle of the night and on weekends. I would threaten to quit therapy just so he could plead with me not to. Twice I even threatened to go to the licensing board. I went as far as writing a formal complaint to the board of psychologists and mailing it. After I did that, I would immediately regret it and have it rescinded. Borderlines are prone to acting impulsively because they cannot handle their feelings. That is why many psychologists shy away from accepting them as their patients, especially ones that work out of their homes. No one will ever forget the movie "Fatal Attraction" when Glen Close boils the pet bunny alive. That movie gave us borderlines a real bad name.

Life with My Schizophrenic Father

Borderlines have deep-seated fear of abandonment.
I had this fear repeatedly in my life. It especially came out whenever I would get close to anyone. That is, I why I seldom had close relationships. This fear especially came up during my intensive therapy with Dick. I was exceptionally vulnerable around the time he would take vacation. And it was painfully hard when he took the whole month of August off. He would call me while he was away and we would exchange emails, but it was nothing like the in-person contact that we shared.

One time after he came back from visiting his in-laws in Denver for a week, I asked him if I could see him that Saturday. I suggested that we go to the local park near where he lived. He was very tired from the long flight back. And on top of that he had a very sore back from sitting in the plane for hours. But he agreed, none the less. It was a beautiful, warm spring day in April. I arrived with my son Austin's football in tow. I sat waiting on the tree stump in his next-door neighbor's front yard. He walked out of his house with a week's worth of stubble on his face, dark sunglasses on, black jeans and sneakers, sporting a wide Cheshire cat grin. We walked to the local park in his neighborhood. It was right behind an elementary school, the one his daughter used to go to.

We tossed the football around and then sat on the grass. He reclined back, propping his head up with his elbows. We didn't say much. This was the most, loving and intimate experience I've ever known. My therapy with Dick would be filled with love and intimacy. He allowed me inside of his home to see his Christmas tree. Even though Dick is Jewish he still bought a Christmas tree every year. I only grew up with fake, tacky artificial trees. I loved the scent and feel and the look of a real one. On the top of his tree instead of a star or an angel he had the sun and the moon. I thought that was appropriate since this man was the sun and the moon to me.

To celebrate our one year of therapy together I made a chocolate cupcake with chocolate frosting and brought it into the session. I placed a large number one candle on top of it. Dick went into his house and brought back milk, glasses and matches to light the candle. We sat on the couch together and blew out the candle. And then I cut the cupcake in half as Dick poured us each a glass of milk. It was such a joyous moment, a real special treat, celebrating my one year of therapy with him.

I had a lot of special moments like that with Dick. On Thursdays I would see Dick for two and a half hours, which gave us plenty of time to do many things. One time he invited me into his workshop. He creates many pieces of furniture with his bare hands. He made the analysis couch in his office, which is much different from a standard couch. (It's much longer) He also made the clock on his wall. I got to see some of the things he was working on and all of the tools that he used to create all these wonderful things that indeed had his personal touch stamped on them. I've been to many, many psychologists over the years but none could compare to the Dick and the love that we shared.

Chapter 13

Living with Mental Illness

My son Alex, my father and I all had one thing in common; we had neurological brain disorders. My son has severe brain damage from contacting meningitis. My father had schizophrenia and I have borderline personality disorder. There are many similarities between all three. I am not a doctor, nor do I have a medical background. I am sharing only what I have lived with, in myself and with my father and son. I want the general public to understand how it is firsthand to have these diseases and mental disorders and how they personally impact your life. They are each very different and yet very similar as well.

I want to talk about the similarity first. Imagine if you will that it's a beautiful sunny day outside. You are out walking and happy with everything. It's warm and the birds are singing. You can smell someone's freshly mowed lawn. Then out of nowhere the sky suddenly turns dark. You see a dark funnel, and the wind is picking up. It's not just going to rain but a tornado is coming straight your way. That tornado is going to destroy everything in its path. You're not prepared at all for this, because just a minute ago it was a beautiful, warm sunny day.

You try to duck for cover, but it's too late. It comes on full throttle upon you without any warning. It's violent and damaging to anything that gets in its path. And you, my dear friend are directly in its path. There is no reasoning to it. It's kind of a madness gone astray.

Life with My Schizophrenic Father

With myself, I usually start feeling intense rage brought on by some perceived hurt that I might not even be aware of now when it's happening. Like if you don't put out your cigarette completely and drop it in the woods. It can start to smolder. That small smolder can turn into a raging forest fire out of control. It engulfs me so much that I want to flee. This is the reason why I have walked off jobs or ended relationship prematurely.

It's similar with my father except that what engulfs him is imagined threats against himself that are simply not true. These threats that somebody wants to hurt him play in his ears. It's like being irrationally scared for no reason after watching a horror movie. It feels like you have headphones on maximum volume that keeps repeating someone is going to kill you in your ear. You can't take the headphones off. And even if you did, you would still hear the voice inside of your head. Sometimes that voice tells you to do bad things. It feels like you are being hypnotized. You have no control over your actions. You are a marionette and the voices control the strings.

With Alex he perseverates on something that gets stuck in his head. He doesn't hear voices like my father, nor does he have imagined hurts like I do. He just obsesses over something and will not relent until he receives it. And he can become extremely violent on his quest for that something. If he wants dinner and dinner is not ready he will repeat the word "dinner" over and over again and not be able to do anything else until he gets it. The longer it goes on the more rage he feels. This can be over anything at any time.

Alex's perseveration is not the same as a spoiled young child's temper-tantrum over not getting what he wants. Severe brain damage causes poor impulse control. Alex is twenty-one years old and perseverates over just about anything. He'll keep saying the same thing over and over again. He might say "mom's twenty-one". He'll get that stuck in his head and won't be able to say or think of anything else. He has faulty neurons going off in his brain because his brain is not wired like a normal person's brain is. The same is true with a person who has schizophrenia and borderline personality disorder. These are diseases that you cannot rationalize with. It doesn't mean that you are hopeless if you have them. With the right therapy and medication, they can be kept under control.

My feelings take over me as much as the voices in my father's head took over him. I always compared myself to a broken thermostat. I'm either boiling hot or completely frozen. There is no middle ground with a borderline. Where the world sees in color, a borderline only sees in black or white. And Alex only sees whatever he is perseverating on. His language is limited to that of a two-year-old, although he does have some comprehension of a child slightly older. My mother was never diagnosed with a mental condition because she never visited a psychologist. But I would say that she had narcissistic personality disorder. It is a condition in which people lack empathy and have exaggerated images of themselves. My mother always said she was the best mother. Her actions never conveyed this.

Living with My Schizophrenic Father

Mental illness can remain hidden. None of my friends knew about my father's condition. I even kept my father's schizophrenia from my future husband, Andrew when we were dating. I didn't even know myself until close to my father's death that his illness had a name. And I didn't know that I was a borderline until my therapy with Dick in 2005 when I was almost forty years old.

The world is full of people wearing masks. You can be next door neighbors with a sociopath and not even know it. All growing up I never knew my cousin Steven was a sociopath. Once I entered therapy, I became completely immersed in it. I deeply regret not taking it up in college. I also began writing poetry and have self-published five poetry books. I think I spent the better part of my life completely dissociated from the real world.

I know that many people don't believe in "labels". But labels helped me put a name to something and gave me a much better understanding of myself and my father. You don't have to solely identify with the label. It only helps you to better understand why you do the things you do. Without that understanding it is hard to stop the behavior. People can have more compassion if they understand that people with mental illness aren't really trying to be hard to get along with. They are people who are suffering a great deal within themselves.

Chapter 14

All Those Years Ago

"Living with good and bad. I always looked up to you." These words from the song "All Those Years Ago", written about John Lennon from former Beatle George Harrison I thought would be appropriate here. My dad and I had some really wild times together that I will never forget. Through it all my father kept his sense of humor. My dad loved sports almost as much as he loved gambling. We both enjoyed baseball. I wanted to surprise my father, so I wrote a long letter to the manager of the Minnesota Twins Sam Mele. I gave him my home phone number and asked him to call my house. I told him that my father was a big sports fan and would love to talk baseball with him. Mele also played for the Boston Red Sox as well as other teams.

Sure, enough one day the phone rang and on the other end of it was Sam Mele!! My father was at his family home, two houses over "on the patio". "The patio" was an outside arena of concrete tables and chairs on a carpet of flagstone where everyone in the family, including the neighbors convened to gossip. I had to run over and tell him that the great Sam Mele himself was on the phone and waiting to talk to him. My father was tickled pink to receive this phone call. I knew that I had made my Father's Day. After all, I owed him for calling my teacher's friend in order to get my teacher's number for me back in high school. Not many fathers would do that. So, I had my chance to talk privately to my crush, Mr. Moche on the phone and my father had his chance to talk to a big name in baseball.

Living with My Schizophrenic Father

My father owned many cars in his lifetime. He always bought them used. He abused his cars pretty badly as well. He never spent money on the regular maintenance of them and inside they were filled up with his leftover cigarette butts. It reeked of smoke and residual ashes were scattered all over the carpets and console. My father was a chain smoker and his hands were stained yellow from his heavy cigarette use.

He had a red Ford Focus that he was cruising around in the beginning of the twenty-first century. He got into an accident and the front hood was completely smashed in so much that you couldn't close it. So, every time he drove it would flap in the breeze. Instead of getting it fixed he tied it down with some rope.

One time we were both driving down to my mothers-in-law house. This was during the time Andrew was staying with them for a week when I was dating Randy. I wanted to reconcile with Andrew and tell him to move back home. I asked my father to drive me there. So, we jumped in his car and started heading down route 1 when all of a sudden the rope let go of the front hood. Now the hood kept flopping up and down, like a duck bobbing for fish in the water. We called it the "quack, quack". We were on a mission to save my marriage and get to my in-law's home so we didn't stop. But my father couldn't see either because the hood was blocking the windshield. I couldn't wear my seatbelt because my father tied it so you couldn't use it. There we were traveling down the highway with my dad totally blind because he never got his dented hood fixed and the rope that had it tied down came off. I thought we were going to get killed for sure on that drive. When we did finally land at my in-laws house my mother-in-law turned us away. So, all that for nothing!!!

All Those Years Ago

My father was crazy, but the good kind of crazy. I used to go to Suffolk Downs racetrack in East Boston with him every now and then. He went there regularly to bet on the horses. A number of famous horses raced there including Sea Biscuit. They made a motion picture about this horse in 2003.He used to study the papers diligently looking up the stats on the horses. I liked to go there just to hang out with my father. I loved watching the horses' race but I didn't gamble. I would instead just drink beer and check out the jockeys.

The only time my mother ever came was when I pleaded with her so we could spend the day as a family. I made my dad promise her a nice Italian dinner at Polcari's . Both my father and I loved to eat, especially Italian food. My mother used to make stuffed artichokes, which were my favorite. She would first steam them and then fill them with homemade breadcrumbs with lots of garlic and olive oil drizzled on top before she baked them in the oven.

My father would often be generous enough to give up his heart. The heart of the artichoke is really the best part and the most work to get at. After you eat all the flesh from the leaves, by scraping it off with your teeth and removing the choke you get to the heart. You never actually eat the leaves, although I have tried as a kid to do just that. The choke is the thistle of thorns that is completely inedible. You must pull that off and discard it to get at the soft, tender sweet meat of the heart. My mother always said that my father loved me the most when he would give up his heart for me, well artichoke heart, that is.

Living with My Schizophrenic Father

That's how my father was with food. He would spend hours peeling the skins off these tiny pearl onions for Thanksgiving. He would peel a dozen of potatoes for the potato stuffing that my mother used to make. He was very patient, and he always enjoyed good food and spent the money on it as well. He would never skimp or cut corners when it came to food.

I remember Sunday afternoons. One o'clock sharp we would have our big "supper". The Italians would eat their big meal in the afternoon. It was the European way. Then they would take it easy the rest of the day. During those days no stores were open on Sundays and people just didn't work. My family never went to church or for that matter really spent time visiting anyone. My mother spent all morning on a Sunday cooking and making homemade spaghetti sauce. She would put all kinds of meats into it and let it slowly simmer. It would come out very flavorful. She never made homemade pasta. But my mother was not Italian. She never really cared about food either like my father did.

The rest of the day and evening was spent lounging around reading the Sunday paper. I always read "the funnies" as I called them. That was the cartoon section. I liked looking at the ads and "The Parade" section as well as the "Tv Week". Times were very simpler back then. My father always raced off to the track after supper and left my mom alone to clean all the dishes. I was guilty as well in not helping her clean up. I always went off to a friend's house.

All Those Years Ago

My father did really well having such a severe disorder as schizophrenia. He held down a job all his life. He never was on a disability. He worked really hard six days a week. And that was very difficult because the drugs that he was on made him severely tired all the time. My mother always complained that if he hadn't gambled, we could have had so much more. But I didn't think we did that bad, although I did grow up with a family of rats in my back yard. The rats were there because there was a meat market right next door to our house called Charlie's Market. I remember stealing a candy bar from that store once as a kid with Charlie, the owner right on my tail chasing me out the door to retrieve it.

In the back of our house there used to be a big hill were all the garbage from the market was dumped. That brought the rats. It was scary. I was terrified of going out in our back yard because there was a half dozen of rats on the prowl. I remember one time helping my mother carry a very full tin trash can to put out on the street when one humongous rat jumped out of it while we had it in tow. The rat touched my arm when it made the jump. I was shaking and crying all day after that. These were not the friendly white rats that you find in the pet stores. These were huge, dingy grey rats that were on the hunt for food, of any and all kinds. I bet a kid's arm would look like a nice loaf of sweet bread to that rat. We also had mice in the house as well. The rodents loved our house. They must have thought that it was the Bates Motel.

Living with My Schizophrenic Father

My father didn't have much in the way of social graces. One time on his birthday when someone said happy birthday to him, he replied "same to you". He wasn't saying it as a joke. I just think he was stumped about what to say back to them. He created the biggest faux pas the night of my rehearsal dinner. Everyone from the wedding party was invited to the church to rehearse for the big day of my wedding. After the rehearsal we had an evening of dining and dancing at Benjamin's Restaurant in Taunton. Everyone was dressed up for the big occasion. My father came dressed in a nice black suit and patent leather black shoes. But underneath the fancy black patent leather shoes he wore thick white, socks, the kind of socks a guy wears under sneakers NOT under fancy dress shoes!!

There were plenty of whispers under the table about what my father had on under his shoes. When he sat down for dinner it was really noticeable because his pants were riding a bit short on him, so short that one might ask "where's the flood?" Of course, my mother was deeply embarrassed. But why hadn't she noticed prior to them leaving? She was probably far too busy getting herself all dolled up. Anyway, a mistake like that is good for a laugh. No one should take themselves so seriously. Besides, he dressed perfectly on my real wedding day. Although I do admit he looked really nervous. My mother appeared totally in control and perfectly dressed in an ivory long laced gown. She wasn't one ounce shy or out of place in social situations. My father and I were more of the wallflowers in the family.

All Those Years Ago

One funny trick I played on my father was the week that Andrew moved into his parent's house. I had Randy come up to stay with me. My father warned me that he didn't want Randy sleeping overnight upstairs when Andrew was away. He said that I was still a married woman. We lived in the same house, so it was hard to sneak Randy in. My mother was doing the dishes and you had to pass her kitchen to come in the back way. She had her kitchen door wide open since it was a summer's evening. So, the only way Randy could come in was through the front. The only problem with that was that my father was cutting the front hedges when Randy arrived.

I don't know how we maneuvered it but Randy snuck by my father while he was doing the hedges. The sound of the hedge cutter would have drowned out any noise that Randy could have possibly made. But still it was hairy. My father could have looked up and saw him sneaking in at any moment. You couldn't miss Randy, since he was a large man. He looked just like Fred Flintstone. In fact, I called him Fred and he called me Dino. My last name after all, is Pall a Dino.
We thought we were lucky escaping that until a short while when my father came upstairs knocking on my door. Randy had to hide. My father came in searching all over the house saying, "you better not have him up here". Luckily, he never found him and left. But deep down I knew that I was not pulling the wool over my father's eyes that time.

Living with My Schizophrenic Father

My father had a few "sayings" or quotes, if you will. I never really understood the logic behind any of them. But they seemed to work for him. One of the things he repeated all my life to me, which I think was meant to be a great lesson was "they can't eat you". Now I don't know exactly what great insight that was. Most people are not cannibals. No one goes around eating other people. I think what he meant by this is what is the worst that can happen to you in a situation? I guess my father never heard about Jeffrey Dahmer.

Another phrase my father would say was "what it, it". Now I have no idea what this actually means. But let me tell you one thing this phrase was sure very catchy. Both my husband and I would get so hooked on it that we kept repeating it "what, it, it". Try it yourself; you just might get hooked too. It was a nonsense thing that made me laugh. My father and I would say these nonsense things, which he would invent and we both would laugh hysterically while it annoyed my mother intensely. He also would sing about one of the voices that he heard in his head, the one named Dreddrew. I'm not sure of the spelling. The little ditty that he would sing would go something like this: "Hey Dreddrew, drew, drew, Hey Dredree, Dree, Dree." There was also some song about the fish Baccala', which is dried and salted cod. It went like this: "Sha la, la, fish a bacca, bacca, la." The Italians have many recipes that they use with this fish. My grandmother cooked the Baccala' in the pasta sauce. My dad also loved tripe. Tripe is the lining of a cow's stomach. Hey, us Italian's will put just about anything in a tomato sauce.

About the Author

I certainly consider myself to be a pariah. I don't hold a job and I've had an open marriage. I write every morning without fail and have very liberal views about things. I consider myself to be a late bloomer. I still feel very much like a child inside, that is why I can relate so well to my son Alex. I don't believe in limitations and I strongly believe in following your dreams.

So much of life is against us; why be against yourself? You will never regret doing what is right for yourself, carving out a happy life in which you are truly free to pursue your own goals and follow your own heart. I grew up in the shadows of my domineering mother. I was extremely shy and very insecure. I didn't know what I wanted to do with my life. I didn't even really know myself. I just went along doing what I thought a person was supposed to do, go to college, get a job and get married. I never asked myself what I really wanted out of life.

My passion is writing. And that is what I do. I have tried to get published, giving up two years of my life to a well-known card company and failed. Now I am no longer waiting and self-publish everything on my own. It's all available on Amazon. At least this way I own all the rights to my own work. It is a dedication of love because I don't get any real monetary value out of it. But too many people equate success with money. To me, success is freedom. I've had traditional jobs that I was miserable doing, jobs that had no meaning, like patrolling the mall as a security guard.

There is something I really want to enforce and encourage of anyone reading this book. Along with following your dreams is the belief that anyone can truly be happy even living with a severe diagnosis such as schizophrenia and brain damage. These are only labels and in no way take away someone's ability to love and to give and to have a rewarding life.

I had the most loving father a girl could have even though he had a very crippling mental illness. He was more patient and kinder and giving of himself more than many fathers who have no challenges. My son is also the most amazing and loving young man I know even though he can't read or write. It doesn't take or subtract from the special times that we have together.

I, myself have had many struggles to. You can't tell what a person is going through just by what they look like on the outside. Too many people are too quick to judge someone they don't even know. I hope this book raises people's awareness of mental illness and that the pathway to happiness is attainable for everyone.

Peace,
Sandra Lee